Drug Abuse

by Hal Marcovitz

LUCENT BOOKS
A part of Gale, Cengage Learning

GALE
CENGAGE Learning™

Detroit • New York • San Francisco • New Haven, Conn • Waterville, Maine • London

LIBRARY OF CONGRESS CATALOGING-IN-PUBLICATION DATA

Marcovitz, Hal.
  Drug abuse / by Hal Marcovitz.
    p. cm. — (Hot topics)
  Includes bibliographical references and index.
  ISBN 978-1-4205-0081-3 (hardcover)
  1. Drug abuse—United States—Juvenile literature. I. Title.
  HV5809.5.M334 2009
  362.290973—dc22

                                                    2008016445

Lucent Books
27500 Drake Rd.
Farmington Hills, MI 48331

ISBN-13: 978-1-4205-0081-3
ISBN-10: 1-4205-0081-3

Printed in the United States of America
1 2 3 4 5 6 7 12 11 10 09 08

CONTENTS

FOREWORD

Young people today are bombarded with information. Aside from traditional sources such as newspapers, television, and the radio, they are inundated with a nearly continuous stream of data from electronic media. They send and receive e-mails and instant messages, read and write online "blogs," participate in chat rooms and forums, and surf the Web for hours. This trend is likely to continue. As Patricia Senn Breivik, the former dean of university libraries at Wayne State University in Detroit, has stated, "Information overload will only increase in the future. By 2020, for example, the available body of information is expected to double every 73 days! How will these students find the information they need in this coming tidal wave of information?"

Ironically, this overabundance of information can actually impede efforts to understand complex issues. Whether the topic is abortion, the death penalty, gay rights, or obesity, the deluge of fact and opinion that floods the print and electronic media is overwhelming. The news media report the results of polls and studies that contradict one another. Cable news shows, talk radio programs, and newspaper editorials promote narrow viewpoints and omit facts that challenge their own political biases. The World Wide Web is an electronic minefield where legitimate scholars compete with the postings of ordinary citizens who may or may not be well-informed or capable of reasoned argument. At times, strongly worded testimonials and opinion pieces both in print and electronic media are presented as factual accounts.

Conflicting quotes and statistics can confuse even the most diligent researchers. A good example of this is the question of whether or not the death penalty deters crime. For instance, one study found that murders decreased by nearly one-third when the death penalty was reinstated in New York in 1995. Death penalty supporters cite this finding to support their argument that the existence of the death penalty deters criminals from committing murder. However, another study found that states without the death penalty have murder rates below the national average. This study is cited by opponents of capital punishment, who reject the claim that the death penalty deters murder. Students need context and clear, informed discussion if they are to think critically and make informed decisions.

The Hot Topics series is designed to help young people wade through the glut of fact, opinion, and rhetoric so that they can think critically about controversial issues. Only by reading and thinking critically will they be able to formulate a viewpoint that is not simply the parroted views of others. Each volume of the series focuses on one of today's most pressing social issues and provides a balanced overview of the topic. Carefully crafted narrative, fully documented primary and secondary source quotes, informative sidebars, and study questions all provide excellent starting points for research and discussion. Full-color photographs and charts enhance all volumes in the series. With its many useful features, the Hot Topics series is a valuable resource for young people struggling to understand the pressing issues of the modern era.

THE NATIONAL TRAGEDY
OF DRUG ABUSE

Each day nearly 4 million Americans abuse drugs. They may be pot smokers, crack cocaine addicts, methamphetamine junkies, or prescription-drug abusers. Despite annual expenditures of billions of dollars by the federal government as well as the states and local communities aimed at wiping out the narcotics trade, drug abuse remains very much a part of the fabric of American society. According to John P. Walters, director of the White House Office of National Drug Control Policy, "Outdated notions casting drug use as a 'recreational' or 'lifestyle' choice have resulted in generations of persistent and ruinous drug use."[1]

Indeed, Americans have abused drugs for decades if not centuries. Marijuana arrived in America with the early colonists. By the nineteenth century, patent medicines containing opiates could be purchased legally for a few cents per bottle. Heroin was first introduced to Americans as an ingredient of aspirin. During the 1960s, psychedelic drugs were found on many college campuses. A decade later, chic cocaine users sniffed the white powder in fashionable discos.

In the meantime, club drugs such as ecstasy and ketamine have found a niche of their own, and crystal meth has become the drug of choice in rural America. A particularly potent form of marijuana, known as chronic, dominates hip-hop culture. In comfortable and otherwise crime-free suburbs, drug abusers break into pharmacies to steal prescription painkillers, which can induce narcotic effects similar to heroin. In professional sports locker rooms, athletes secretly dope themselves with steroids and other illegal performance-enhancing drugs as they seek an edge over their competitors.

The list of drugs and how they can be abused seems to be endless. Nora Volkow, director of the National Institute on Drug Abuse, explains, "The use of drugs has been recorded since the beginning of civilization. Humans in my view will always want to experiment with things that make them feel good."[2]

Victories and Defeats

Given the overwhelming problem of drug abuse, authorities can do little but point to small victories and hope their message is being heard. For example, between 2002 and 2006 the use of marijuana among young people between the ages of twelve and seventeen declined from 8.2 percent to 6.7 percent. U.S. Health

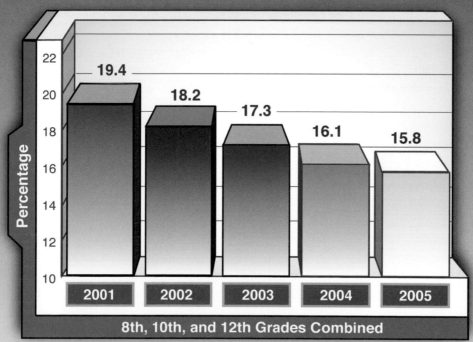

Students Reporting Past Month Use of Any Illicit Drug Has Decreased

19 Percent Decline 2001 to 2005[*]

- 2001: 19.4
- 2002: 18.2
- 2003: 17.3
- 2004: 16.1
- 2005: 15.8

Percentage

8th, 10th, and 12th Grades Combined

Taken from: University of Michigan, 2005 Monitoring the Future Study.
www.drugabuse.gov/newsroom/05/images/slide1.jpg

[*]P<.05

and Human Services secretary Mike Leavitt believes the decline is due to the effectiveness of national and community-based antidrug programs. "The trends in general are very encouraging," Leavitt says. "Parents and communities are doing a great job helping more and more children make the right choice when it comes to illicit drug abuse."[3]

On the other hand, in the drug wars it is not unusual to find victories accompanied by defeats. While the use of marijuana seems to have declined among young people, the abuse of prescription drugs is on the rise. According to the U.S. Substance Abuse and Mental Health Services Administration, prescription-drug abuse among fourteen-year-olds rose from 6.9 percent in 2005 to 8.4 percent in 2006; for fifteen-year-olds, abuse of prescription drugs rose from 9.9 percent in 2005 to 11.5 percent in 2006. Experts have theorized that teenagers are stealing pills from their parents' medicine cabinets.

Meanwhile, Americans tend to send mixed signals about drugs. In 2007, a poll by the Gallup Organization found that 73 percent of Americans regard the problem of drug abuse as very serious. Yet other polls have shown that some 40 percent of American adults have admitted to using marijuana at some point in their lives, and that the number of people who believe marijuana should be legalized has climbed in recent years. A 2005 Gallup poll found that 36 percent of Americans favor legalization of marijuana; a decade before, 25 percent of Americans favored legalizing pot.

Across-the-board legalization of illicit drugs is not likely to occur in the foreseeable future. Few politicians can be expected to put their careers on the line by advocating the legalization of substances that are easily abused and have, in most cases, proven to be harmful to people's health. In 1993, U.S. surgeon general Joycelyn Elders suggested that the federal government should study the legalization of drugs as a way of reducing crime. Her boss, President Bill Clinton, reacted coldly to the idea. Eventually, he fired her. Later, Elders modified her position—after her son, Kevin, was arrested for selling cocaine. According to Elders, prison probably saved Kevin's life by making him quit drugs. "Now, he's addicted to work and making money, so I guess that's all right,"[4] Elders says.

For Americans, the cost of drugs does not end at the staggering price tag taxpayers spend to keep them out of the hands of abusers. Even after all those billions of dollars are spent on policing the illegal drug trade, hundreds of millions more must be spent on prisons for dealers and traffickers, recovery programs for addicts, and health care for people whose years of addiction have ruined their bodies. Meanwhile, there are other costs that cannot be measured in dollars: the costs of broken families, ruined futures, and wasted lives invariably caused by drug addiction.

DRUG ABUSE
IN AMERICA

Marijuana, which is also known as cannabis, has been a part of human culture for some four thousand years. The first known use of the drug was recorded in the Atharva Veda, an ancient Hindu text written two thousand years before the birth of Christ. Over the centuries, the ancient Greeks were known to smoke and eat the plant. Many biblical scholars believe there are references to marijuana in the Old Testament. For example, the word *honeywood* in the first book of Samuel may be a reference to marijuana. Eventually the plant found its way to Europe; archaeologists have unearthed an urn in Germany, believed to be some twenty-five hundred years old, that contains the remnants of marijuana leaves and seeds.

Marijuana first arrived in America aboard the ships that carried the first settlers to the New World. The fiber from the plants was spun into hemp, which was used to manufacture rope, fabric, and sails. In making hemp, the leafy part of the plant, which contains the narcotic content, was discarded. Most hemp growers—including George Washington—were known to discard the leaves, but at some point in the young history of the colonies somebody obviously came upon the revelation that when smoked, the leaves of the cannabis plant could provide a dreamy, euphoric feeling. In 1851 the *United States Dispensatory*, a reference book for pharmacists, warned, "Extract of hemp is a powerful narcotic . . . causing exhilaration, intoxication, delirious hallucinations, and, in its subsequent action, drowsiness and stupor."[5]

The introduction of marijuana to the colonies marked the beginning of a long relationship between drug use and American society. Despite all the trends that have come and gone in America; despite all the wars that have been fought; despite all the advancements in the arts and sciences; despite all the changes in political climate, fashion, hairstyles, and music, the one constant in American society has always been that somewhere, somebody is getting high.

POT AND THE POET

"Allen opened a big file cabinet and pulled out reports for me to read on the medical, legal, and historical aspects of cannabis sativa. He was eager to help anyone who would write objectively about this drug he believed should be legalized."

Author Dan Wakefield describing a meeting with Beat poet Allen Ginsberg in 1961. Dan Wakefield, *New York in the 50s.* New York: Houghton Mifflin, 1992, p. 177.

Patent Medicines

Marijuana was not the only illicit drug that found widespread use in America. During the 1850s Chinese immigrants introduced Americans to the custom of smoking opium. Chinese laborers were employed by the tens of thousands to build the western railroads. At night, as they rested in their camps, the Chinese workers smoked opium to ease the pain from the day's grueling labors. Soon others were smoking opium as well. The practice became so widespread that, in 1875, the city of San Francisco outlawed opium parlors. According to H.H. Kane, a New York doctor who was the country's leading authority on opium during the nineteenth century, "Many women and young girls, as well as young men of respectable family, were being induced to visit [Chinese opium-smoking] dens, where they were ruined morally and otherwise."[6]

Actually, Americans did not have to sneak into illegal opium dens to use narcotics. Patent medicines that purported to eliminate headaches, ease sore throats, and settle queasy stomachs often contained opiates as ingredients. Such products as Mrs. Winslow's Soothing Syrup, McMunn's Elixir of Opium, and Darby's

Chinese immigrants introduced Americans to opium smoking and opened opium dens, where smokers could indulge the habit.

Carminative were sold by salesmen door to door, were available on the shelves of pharmacies, and were advertised widely in the newspapers of the era. Likewise, the companies that manufactured the elixirs and syrups did not have to go through the bother or expense of importing the opium from the Far East. During the nineteenth century, opium was a cash crop in many of the southern states.

By the early 1900s, many leading physicians of the era concluded that patent medicines were either worthless or harmful. Harvey W. Wiley, a physician and chief chemist for the U.S. Agriculture Department, became a zealous advocate for outlawing patent medicines. In 1906 Wiley and other experts convinced Congress to pass the Pure Food and Drug Act, which set strict requirements on how medicines could be manufactured and distributed. The act also required drugmakers to list the contents on the bottles. The fly-by-night patent medicine companies, unable to meet the new federal standards, soon went out of business.

The act did not specifically outlaw narcotics, but by then many of the states had passed antidrug laws of their own. Still, there was pressure on the federal level to take action, mainly because many other countries were struggling with their own narcotics addiction problems. Their leaders hoped an international strategy could be developed. In 1909 and 1911, the United States

Coca-Cola and Cocaine

Coca-Cola, one of the most popular soft drinks in America, was originally formulated in 1886 by patent medicine manufacturer John Styth Pemberton. Pemberton produced the drink in syrup form as a medicine, marketing it as a "remarkable therapeutic agent." As part of the formula, Pemberton included extract of coca leaves, which he imported from South America. Extract of coca leaves is the ingredient of cocaine that provides the illegal drug with its narcotic kick.

By the early 1900s the formula had been obtained by pharmacist Asa Candler, who transformed the product into a soft drink, but he also touted its ability to relieve headaches and other ailments. In 1909 Coca-Cola came to the attention of Harvey W. Wiley, who by then had taken over the U.S. Bureau of Food and Drugs. Wiley filed a lawsuit against Coca-Cola, charging that the company violated the Pure Food and Drug Act by including extract of coca leaves in the formula. The case dragged through the courts for many years, but in 1918 the company settled the suit by agreeing to change the formula and market the product solely as a soft drink.

Quoted in Edward M. Brecher, *Licit and Illicit Drugs: The Consumer Union Report.* New York: Consumers Union, 1972, p. 270.

sent diplomats to international opium conferences, which were called to address the burgeoning Far East drug trade. Meeting in Belgium in late 1911, the diplomats drafted the 1912 International Opium Convention, which required the member nations to "enact effective laws or regulations for the control of the production and distribution of raw opium."[7] In response, Congress passed the 1914 Harrison Narcotics Act, which placed strict controls on the opiate content of most drugs and made it illegal to sell opiates to drug addicts.

Harry J. Anslinger and the Federal Bureau of Narcotics

Despite the new law, by 1919 the campaign against illegal drug use in America had become much less of a priority. That was the year the states ratified the Eighteenth Amendment to the U.S. Constitution, outlawing the manufacture and sale of alcoholic beverages. On January 16, 1920, Prohibition went into effect; for

Harry J. Anslinger became the first director of the Federal Bureau of Narcotics. His first campaign was to make marijuana illegal.

the next thirteen years, the resources of the federal government were committed to the largely futile task of smashing bootlegging rings, nabbing moonshiners and rumrunners, and rooting out the thousands of speakeasies that were hidden in cities throughout the country. While federal agents hunted down such big-time bootleggers as Al Capone, drug use flourished in America.

THE MADNESS OF MARIJUANA

"Those addicted to marihuana, after an early feeling of exhilaration, soon lose all restraints, all inhibitions. They become bestial demoniacs, filled with the mad lust to kill."

United News Service journalist Kenneth Clark, profiling the marijuana trade in 1936. Quoted in Larry Sloman, *Reefer Madness: A History of Marijuana*. New York: St. Martin's Griffin, 1998, p. 48.

In 1930, with Prohibition stumbling to a close, Congress redirected some of the resources devoted to alcohol enforcement to investigating drug traffickers. Two years later Congress created the Federal Bureau of Narcotics, appointing former Prohibition agent Harry J. Anslinger as the first director. Anslinger soon called for a federal law banning the use of marijuana. Anslinger traveled the country calling for a war on marijuana and wrote many articles for leading American magazines describing the horrors of the drug. Writing in a 1937 issue of *American Magazine*, Anslinger described what he said was a typical marijuana experience:

> In Los Angeles, Calif., a youth was walking along a downtown street after inhaling a marihuana cigarette. For many addicts, merely a portion of a "reefer" is enough to induce intoxication. Suddenly, for no reason, he decided that someone had threatened to kill him and that his life at that very moment was in danger. Wildly he looked about him. The only person in sight was an aged bootblack [person who shines shoes]. Drug-crazed nerve centers conjured the innocent old shoe-shiner into a destroying monster. Mad with fright, the addict hurried to his room and got a gun. He killed the old man, and then, later, babbled his grief over what had been wanton, uncontrolled murder.[8]

Egged on by such rhetoric, Congress adopted the Marijuana Tax Act of 1937, which assessed heavy fees on hemp farmers and outlawed recreational use of the drug. The tax on hemp farmers was so heavy that few could afford to pay the levies, and within a few years the hemp business in America disappeared. As for the illegal users of the crop, Anslinger's agents made their first arrests within eight days of the adoption of the act.

The Federal Bureau of Narcotics continued to arrest drug users and dealers with fervor, but with fascism growing in Europe and Japan, the drug war was once again relegated to a low priority. Indeed, Americans would soon be engaged in fighting a far different type of war.

Turn On, Tune In, Drop Out

Following World War II, a new generation of Americans discovered drugs. Many people in the public eye were known drug users, including writers Jack Kerouac and Allen Ginsberg; movie stars Robert Mitchum and Montgomery Clift; musicians John Coltrane, Charlie Parker, and Chet Baker; and singer Billie Holiday. Meanwhile, some veterans of the Korean War had gotten hooked on a combination of amphetamines and heroin known as "speedballs." When they returned to the United States, they turned to a prescription drug to feed their habits: methamphetamine, a pain medication known on the streets as "speed" or "crank." In 1963, alarmed at the widespread use of methamphetamine as an illegal substance, federal regulators placed strict regulations on the use of the drug. Those rules hardly dented the speed trade; underground labs soon found ways to make the drug on their own. The drug became the substance of choice for outlaw motorcycle gangs, which took over the manufacture and delivery of speed. Eventually the U.S. Justice Department would charge thirty-two members of the Hell's Angels motorcycle gang with running an extensive speed distribution ring. "The cornerstone of this illegal drug enterprise was the large-scale manufacture and mass distribution of methamphetamine,"[9] says U.S. attorney G. William Hunter.

Meanwhile, in the new suburbs that were growing around cities, teenagers and other young people discovered they could

Los Angeles County Sheriff officers search members of the Hells Angel's motorcycle gang for illegal drugs.

experience a mind-numbing rush by sniffing model airplane glue, which they could buy in any hobby store for a few cents. The high-inducing ingredient in the glue is toluene, a solvent that helps the glue dry faster. Doctors started looking at the fad and concluded that it was very dangerous: Glue-sniffing could cause permanent damage to the brain, kidneys, and liver. The model airplane glue industry addressed the problem, and by the late 1960s manufacturers added ingredients to the glue that makes sniffers gag if they try to inhale the fumes. However, that has not deterred most people who wish to abuse inhalants. To-day there are hundreds of products available on the shelves of supermarkets and hardware stores that contain toluene or other solvents that can provide a high.

Drugs were also finding their way onto college campuses. The 1960s represented an era of great rebellion in American

Drugs and the Vietnam War

Nearly 3 million Americans served in the Vietnam War between 1964 and 1975. Many of them found easy access to drugs and returned to the United States as addicts. In 1971 a congressional study found that drugs in Vietnam were "more plentiful than cigarettes and chewing gum." Another study suggested that the war had created some thirty thousand heroin addicts.

By far, the most plentiful drug found in Vietnam was marijuana. During the war military leaders expressed constant concern that discipline in the ranks had eroded because of rampant marijuana use. Vietnam veteran Bob Franco says:

The only drugs I actually saw men taking was maybe smoking grass. A little marijuana on a three-day stand-out. Now, what I would do is when we came back for a three-day rest before going on another operation, I would just say to the men, 'Look, go get drunk. . . . If you're gonna smoke a little dope, don't get caught.' They'd always show up on the third day straight . . . because they knew out in the field anybody that wasn't alert they could cost the other guy's life.

Quoted in Vietnam Online, "Vietnamizing the War," *American Experience*. www.pbs.org/wgbh/amex/vietnam/series/pt_07.html.

society: the civil rights movement, women's rights movement, and other social changes prompted young people to exert their independence from their parents. Indeed, their independence could be found in their hair and clothing styles, their opposition to the Vietnam War, their advocacy of free love, and their desire to use drugs. By the 1960s marijuana had become a common drug found at most universities in America. Another drug found on campuses was lysergic acid diethylamide (LSD), one of the so-called psychedelic drugs that cause users to experience vivid hallucinations. LSD and similar psychedelic drugs were available in neighborhoods such as Haight-Ashbury in San Francisco and Greenwich Village in New York. One of the most significant spokesmen for the drug movement in the 1960s was Timothy Leary, a former Harvard University professor who believed LSD expanded the minds of users, opening their consciousness to all manner of new ideas and experiences. In his biography, *Turn On, Tune In, Drop Out*, Leary writes:

You are a spiritual voyager furthering the most ancient, noble quest of man. When you turn on, you . . . join the holy dance of visionaries.

To turn on, you need a sacrament. A sacrament is a visible eternal thing which turns the key to the inner doors. A sacrament must bring about bodily changes. A sacrament flips you out . . . and harnesses you to the 2-billion-year-old flow inside. . . .

Today the sacrament is LSD. New sacraments are coming along.

Sacraments wear out. . . . Treasure LSD while it still works. In fifteen years it will be tame, socialized, and routine.[10]

Former Harvard professor Timothy Leary became an advocate of LSD during the 1960s.

By the late 1960s and early 1970s, drug use was firmly established as a major element of popular culture. Comedians such as George Carlin, Cheech and Chong, and the Smothers Brothers peppered their acts with drug references. The 1969 film *Easy Rider* tells the story of two drug dealers crossing America on their motorcycles; it was one of the most successful films of the year. On the Broadway stage, the musical *Hair* chronicled the bohemian lifestyle of hippie culture, and several songs from the play described drug use. The show was one of the biggest hits of 1968. Recording stars Arlo Guthrie, Bob Dylan, Jimi Hendrix, and Jefferson Airplane released albums with songs that romanticized their use of drugs. In 1969 a half-million young people attended the Woodstock rock festival in upstate New York; drug use was so rampant that documentary cameras caught many festival goers and performers using substances. Drug use was so widespread at the festival that the stage announcer found it necessary to issue warnings about tainted drugs circulating in the crowd. One of the most successful books of 1971 was *Fear and Loathing in Las Vegas*, which recounts the experiences of a sportswriter as he spends a weekend in Las Vegas stoned on a variety of illegal substances. Entering a hotel lobby in the midst of an LSD hallucination, author Hunter S. Thompson sees nothing but a roomful of lizards. "My legs felt rubbery," writes Thompson. "I gripped the desk and sagged toward her as she held out the envelope, but I refused to accept it. The woman's face was changing: swelling, pulsing . . . horrible green jowls and fangs jutting out, the face of a moray eel! Deadly poison!"[11]

Chronic and Crystal Meth

As the 1970s moved on, the disco music craze gave rise to cocaine use. Hip celebrities and others gathered at chic discos where they took turns sniffing the white powder through rolled-up dollar bills. Anybody who doubted what was going on need only look at the neon sign hanging at the entrance of the hippest disco in New York, Studio 54. The sign included an image of the man in the moon inhaling cocaine from a spoon. As the celebrities gathered around the coke tables, they snorted the drug, happily oblivious to the truth—that their cocaine was being supplied by vicious and murderous drug cartels operating in Colombia and other Latin American countries. In his book *Snowblind*, writer Robert Sabbag describes the small Colombian port town of Santa Maria, from which cocaine was regularly shipped to the United States:

> Colombian dope, overnight, had become a growth industry. Like every fishing village along the coast, Santa Maria had come alive, and was throwing all its resources behind the national effort. At least two nights a week the local power plant would shut down while the smugglers, by cover of darkness, took their cash-crop cargoes aboard and shipped out. Police bribes were the savings bonds of the nationwide drive.[12]

SCREAMING FOR HOURS

"I tried ecstasy for the first time on Halloween. I was dancing to a tribal house mix of K.D. Lang's 'Lifted by Love' and it sounded like a voice coming down from heaven. I was smiling from one side of my face to the other and remember screaming for about four hours."

Troy Roberts, a rave DJ from Seattle, Washington. Quoted in Jimi Fritz, *Rave Culture: An Insider's Overview*. Victoria, BC: Smallfry, 1999, p. 140.

Pressured by the United States and other countries, Colombia started cleaning up the drug cartels in the 1980s. Still, much cocaine was making its way into the United States, particularly to the inner cities, where it was made available in a cheap version known as crack. More affluent buyers preferred ecstasy, ketamine, and the other so-called club drugs, which dominated the American and European rave scenes. Ecstasy (also known as MDMA for its chemical name, 3,4-methylenedioxymethamphetamine) and the other club drugs provide users with dreamy, euphoric episodes. They can also prompt hallucinations. Moreover, ketamine and other club drugs, such as Rohypnol and gamma hydroxybutyrate (GHB), can cause users to fall into drowsy states; as such, they have been used as date-rape drugs. Assailants have distracted women at parties, dropped the pills into their drinks, and then sexually assaulted them while they were under the influence. In 2000 Andrew Luster, an heir to a cosmetic company fortune, was convicted on twenty counts of date rape. Police charged him with lacing the drinks of three women with heavy doses of GHB and then raping them. One of the victims later described her encounter with Luster: "I didn't know I passed out. All I remember is that I was feeling different, and then I woke up the next day in his bed. I was upset and I asked him what was going on, and he said, 'Don't you remember?' Then he said nothing happened."[13] In 2003 Luster was sentenced to more than one hundred years in prison.

Andrew Luster, heir to the Max Factor cosmetics fortune, is arrested on charges of date rape. He was later convicted.

While the new, trendy drugs like ecstasy and crack found their clienteles, some old standbys were finding new users as well. For example, denizens of hip-hop culture turned on to chronic, a particularly potent strain of marijuana. In 1992 rap star Dr. Dre released one of the year's most successful albums, titled *The Chronic*. As the name suggests, the album features many songs praising the qualities of Dre's drug of choice. Other hip-hop stars who have built their followings largely on their appeal to pot-smoking audiences are Snoop Dogg and Flavor Flav. In 2005 country singer Willie Nelson paid tribute to the late 1970s Jamaican reggae star Bob Marley—whose music was very influenced by the marijuana he smoked—by releasing an album titled *Countryman*. Nelson's CD of reggae songs featured a marijuana plant on its cover. Nelson, by the way, has never denied using marijuana. In the 1970s he boasted of smoking pot on the roof of the White House, where he had been invited to stay by President Jimmy Carter.

DISTRESS SIGNALS

"The euphoric effects of [ecstasy] can distract users from noticing the physical changes or distress signals from their bodies. With a lessened awareness of pain, it is easy to sustain minor bodily injuries and not be aware of it until the following day."

Cynthia R. Knowles, psychotherapist and author. Cynthia R. Knowles, *Up All Night: A Closer Look at Club Drugs and Rave Culture*. New York: Red House, 2001, p. 46.

Meanwhile, in rural areas—but certainly in cities and suburbs as well—amateur drugmakers found a way to make a potent form of methamphetamine, mostly from ingredients available in drugstores and supermarkets. Crystal meth, considered much more powerful than the illegal version of the drug manufactured in the 1960s and 1970s, soon became a plague on America, rising to a top place on the list of the nation's most abused drugs.

Elaborate Tunnels

Much of the crystal meth consumed in America is made in basement labs or in similar, out-of-the-way manufacturing operations.

How Drugs Affect the Brain, the Body, and Behavior

According to the U.S. Centers for Disease Control and Prevention, drug abuse contributes to more than thirty thousand deaths a year. Some drug abusers take accidental overdoses and die suddenly. Indeed, it seems as though every few months the newspapers carry headlines about a celebrity who has died of a drug overdose. Over the years such stars as model Anna Nicole Smith, comedian Chris Farley, basketball player Len Bias, and musician Jimi Hendrix have been found dead, victims of accidental overdoses. And many of these deaths can be ugly: Hendrix, perhaps the greatest rock guitarist of his era, drowned in his own vomit while in a drug-induced stupor.

In the case of actor Heath Ledger, the film star was found dead in his New York City apartment in early 2008. Already one of the brightest young stars in the movies, the twenty-eight-year-old Australian suffered from pain as a result of taking on physically challenging roles. He also had difficulty sleeping and was clinically depressed. And so, shortly before Ledger died, he was known to be consuming no fewer than six prescription medications—drugs to help him sleep, relieve his pain, and alter his moods. The mixture of drugs proved deadly: They slowed down the functions of his organs, particularly his lungs. "His breathing probably got slower and slower until it stopped altogether," says pathologist Michael Hunter. As a result, Hunter says, Ledger died of "poly-drug intoxication."[16]

In others victims, drugs take their toll much more slowly, gradually destroying the vital functions of the brain and body.

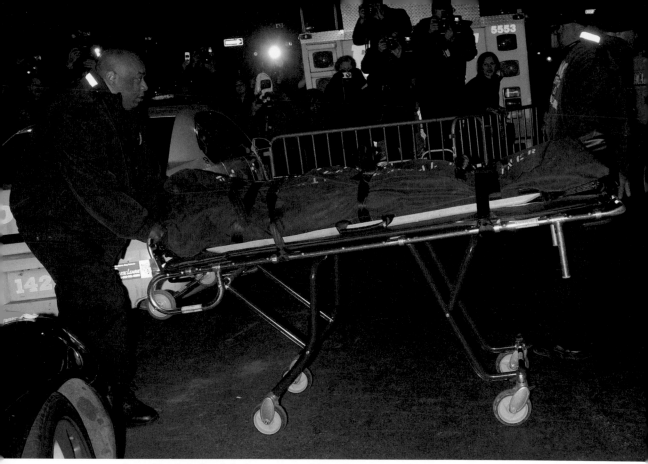

Actor Heath Ledger's body is removed from his New York apartment. He died after taking a mixture of six prescription drugs.

When jazz musician Charlie Parker was found dead of a drug overdose in 1955 the coroner estimated his age at between fifty and sixty. In reality, Parker was only thirty-four years old.

The Effects on Neurotransmitters

Drugs affect many parts of the body, but the primary organ that is impacted by narcotics is the brain. The brain is composed of millions of cells, which are also known as neurons. Each neuron emits an electrical impulse that carries the brain's messages— perhaps instructing the foot to take a step, the lips to form words, or the fingers to grasp a pencil. Within each neuron are a series of stems that act as pathways for the impulses. The larger stems are known as axons; at the end of the axons are smaller stems known as dendrites. The impulse travels along the axon and into the dendrite. When the impulse reaches the end of the dendrite, it must leap over a tiny space known as a synapse on its way to the next dendrite. To enable the electrical impulse to make the leap, the brain produces chemicals known as neurotransmitters, which carry the messages from brain cell to brain cell. On the end of each neuron's dendrite is a group of molecules known as receptors, which accept specific neurotransmitters and transmit the impulse into the neuron and over the next synapse. Not all neurotransmitters carry messages; some prevent unwanted messages from passing from neuron to neuron.

The method the brain employs to communicate with the rest of the body is well synchronized, delicate, and spontaneous. When drugs are introduced into the brain's system of communication, the results can be quite advantageous to the user. Prescription painkillers, when used properly, can block the neurotransmitters that carry messages of pain to the rest of the body.

An electrical impulse from the human brain crosses a synapse. Synapses are made possible by chemicals known as neurotransmitters. Some drugs are able to inhibit pain responses by manipulating the synapses of the brain.

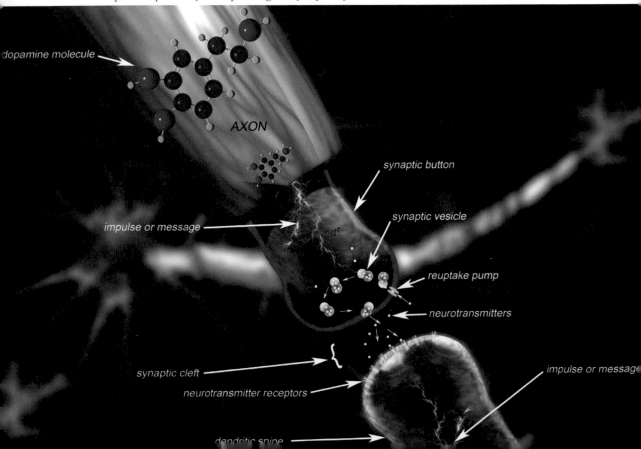

dopamine molecule

AXON

synaptic button

impulse or message

synaptic vesicle

reuptake pump

neurotransmitters

synaptic cleft

impulse or message

neurotransmitter receptors

dendritic spine

Drugs, however, also can be quite disruptive, affecting mood and emotion or motor activity—how a person walks, talks, or operates machinery.

Drugs affect neurotransmitters. Sometimes drugs cause the brain cells to produce too many neurotransmitters, which overwhelm the brain with information. For example, the neurotransmitter dopamine controls motor ability. When people's brains are overloaded with dopamine, they tend to stumble and lose coordination. That is why people who abuse drugs should not drive while they are under the influence of substances.

Inner Peace

"Ecstasy has made me more peaceful with myself and has taught me the extent to which love can be experienced. I never thought that I could feel that much love and positive affection."

Raevn Lunah Teak, an ecstasy user from Brisbane, Australia. Quoted in Jimi Fritz, *Rave Culture: An Insider's Overview.* Victoria, BC: Smallfry, 1999, p. 140.

Neurotransmitters can also alter moods and produce feelings of pleasure. In addition to motor activity, dopamine also controls cognitive thinking, motivation, emotion, and feelings of pleasure—all functions that can be affected by drugs. Some drugs spark the brain to produce more dopamine, enhancing pleasure. That is why drug abusers often feel euphoric and giddy, even though they are stumbling on their feet or crashing into furniture. Methamphetamine and cocaine produce an overwhelming amount of dopamine. "It produces a marked decrease in hunger, an indifference to pain, and is reputed to be the most potent anti-fatigue agent known," writes Jerome H. Jaffe, one of the first medical researchers to assess the narcotic effects of cocaine. "The user enjoys a feeling of great muscular strength and increased mental capacity and greatly overestimates his capabilities. The euphoria is accompanied by generalized . . . stimulation."[17]

Sometimes drugs block neurotransmitters by affecting the receptors. In each brain cell, the neurotransmitters act as keys that unlock specific receptors, which accept the messages and pass them on to the next cell. However, some drugs mimic neurotransmitters, blocking the natural chemicals from entering the receptors. Instead, the drugs take the place of the neurotransmitters and enter the receptors. LSD blocks the neurotransmitter serotonin from finding its proper receptors. Serotonin regulates mood, sleep, pain, emotion, and appetite. Instead of receiving serotonin, the brain absorbs a dose of LSD and its hallucination-causing qualities. The chemical delta-9-tetrahydrocannabinol (THC) is the component of marijuana that provides the narcotic effect. THC is known to block serotonin and take its place in the brain's serotonin receptors. That is why marijuana smokers undergo a change in their moods. Most users experience dreamy, euphoric highs. Marijuana users also notice a change in their appetites. Many pot smokers find themselves famished and ready to gorge on food.

Addictive Qualities

Eventually the brain will grow accustomed to the new sensations provided by the drugs and will create a desire within the user to want more. Most people possess a natural tendency to want more of what gives them pleasure—that is why many people enjoy ice cream more than string beans. Therefore, many people who have tried marijuana, cocaine, ecstasy, or other drugs return for a second dose because of the pleasure they received from their first experiences with the substance.

THE CHANCES OF ADDICTION

"If we can get a child to 20 without using marijuana, there is a 98 percent chance that the child will never become addicted to any drug. While it may come across as an overemphasis on marijuana, you don't wake up when you're 25 and say, 'I want to slam meth!'"

Scott Burns, deputy director of the White House Office of National Drug Control Policy. Quoted in David J. Jefferson, "America's Most Dangerous Drug," *Newsweek*, August 8, 2005, p. 40.

When the brain rewards the body, it releases dopamine. For example, when the body consumes a bowl of ice cream, the brain will respond by releasing a small amount of dopamine, giving

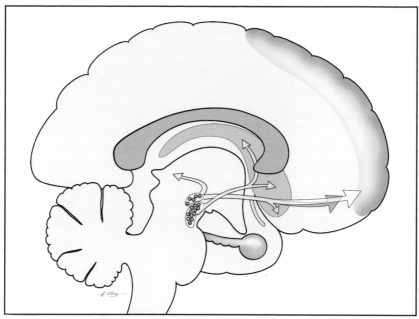

An illustration depicts the dopamine pathways in the brain, showing the origin and distribution of dopamine. Some drugs produce a large amount of dopamine, creating a feeling of pleasure and contentment.

the eater pleasure for having consumed a tasty food. Some drugs prompt the body to release dopamine in amounts ten times the normal quantity. Therefore, the rush of pleasure associated with drug abuse can be enormous. Author and ecstasy abuser Olivia Gordon describes the pleasure she received from the drug as overwhelming. She says, "I felt the rush come on with a moment of joy. . . . Then suddenly I was drowning in a tsunami. It was a rush, but more than a rush. I was burning up. My heart was bursting, accelerating, I couldn't walk, my breath became one long inhalation. . . . My horizon went black and at the same time threads of colors shot like electricity into my head."[18]

The pleasurable experience gained through drugs will also last much longer than the feeling of pleasure produced through a natural release of dopamine. Indeed, the rush of pleasure someone may receive from eating a bowl of ice cream may last no longer than a few seconds or a few minutes, but when prompted by drugs the feelings of pleasure can last much longer. The high produced by cocaine can last thirty minutes or more. People who consume ketamine, which is a hallucinogenic club drug, expect their highs to last for a few hours. Abusers of methamphetamine can expect to stay high and euphoric for twenty-four hours or even several days. "The effect of such a powerful reward strongly motivates people to take drugs again and again," states the National Institutes of Health publication *The Science of Addiction*. "This is why scientists sometimes say drug abuse is something we learn to do very, very well."[19]

The frequent use of drugs often creates an addiction in the user. Over time, the brain has come to rely on the pleasurable sensations provided by drugs, creating a craving in the user for larger and more frequent doses. Gordon found that after she started using ecstasy, a single dose of the drug was no longer capable of getting her high. "Each time I took a pill, the high was getting less glorious,"[20] she says.

In addition, when drugs induce the brain to create more dopamine, the brain stops producing dopamine on its own. That means the brain becomes addicted to drugs to carry out functions it formerly did on its own. Essentially, the only time habitual drug abusers feel good about themselves is when they are using drugs. At other times, their brains simply do not produce dopamine. According to *The Science of Addiction*:

> This is why the abusers eventually feel flat, lifeless and depressed, and are unable to enjoy things that previously brought them pleasure. Now, they need to take drugs just to bring their dopamine function back to normal. And, they must take larger amounts of the drug than they first did to create the dopamine high—an effect known as tolerance.[21]

The National Institutes of Health regards drug addiction as a disease of the brain. As the abuser takes more and more drugs, the way the brain works will change. Its functions have become abnormal. In fact, brain imaging studies performed on long-term drug abusers show that, in many cases, the brain has actually undergone physical changes. After years of drug abuse, the parts of the brain that control judgment, decision making, learning, memory, and behavioral control have shown deterioration.

The saddest fact about addiction is that, in time, most people do arrive at the realization that drugs are bad for them, and yet it is very difficult for them to stop abusing substances. As Joseph Frascella, director of clinical neuroscience at the National Institute of Drug Abuse, explains, "Addictions are repetitive behaviors in the face of negative consequences, the desire to continue something you know is bad for you."[22]

Hijacking Their Judgment

"It's impossible to overstate the hold it has—crack's like baby food compared to meth. It addicts folks, on average, the third time they use it and permanently hijacks their judgment. They don't sleep for weeks, they defecate on the floor and let their kids starve and go naked."

Lyn Eul, drug prevention coordinator for the Snohomish County, Washington, prosecutor's office. Quoted in Paul Soloaroff, "Plague in the Heartland," *Rolling Stone*, January 23, 2003, p. 48.

As their drug use continues, abusers may find themselves experiencing difficulty concentrating, solving problems, and maintaining their short- and long-term memories. Numerous studies have looked at the effects of drugs on cognitive development, and most have concluded that drugs harm the brain. Inhalants, for example, contain harsh industrial chemicals that were never intended to be absorbed directly into the body. When inhaled, these chemicals enter the bloodstream and flow through the brain, where they become lodged in the myelin, the fatty coating of tissue that protects each neuron. Eventually they will break down the myelin, which could damage the neurons or prevent them from transmitting messages. As a result, the drug abuser may find it harder to remember things. As for marijuana, many studies have linked pot to long-term memory loss. In 2005 a five-year study at Johns Hopkins University in Baltimore, Maryland, found that pot causes a reduction in the blood vessels that feed the brain. With less blood in the brain, the brain deteriorates and has more difficulty carrying out its functions. "In the long-term, one might

Abusing Caffeine

Caffeine is a natural-occurring drug found in coffee beans, kola nuts, tea leaves, and other plants. In addition to coffee and tea, caffeine is a key ingredient of chocolate, soft drinks, and energy drinks. Caffeine can provide a person with a brief burst of energy and help stave off sleep. Caffeine blocks the neurotransmitter adenosine, which helps slow down the brain and body and enables people to rest.

Caffeine also has addictive qualities—some people simply must have a cup of coffee in the morning. The nineteenth-century French author Honoré de Balzac was extremely addicted to caffeine. When he found that the numerous cups of strong, syrupy black coffee that he con-sumed each day failed to give him the rush he desired, he started grinding up coffee beans and eating them.

The drug can also be abused. Athletes have been known to consume huge quantities of caffeine before competitions in the belief that the drug will provide them with deep reservoirs of energy. In 2001 Minnesota Vikings lineman Korey Stringer died of heatstroke after practicing on a particularly hot day. Before practice, Stringer consumed pills containing caffeine and ephedra, another energy-producing drug. Both substances are known to cause dehydration, which was a contributing factor in Stringer's death.

In a humorous photograph, a businessman takes part of his coffee intravenously.

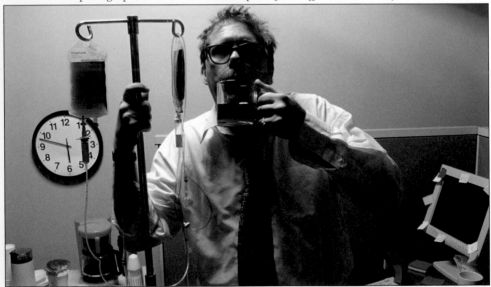

see cognitive difficulties, such as problems with memory and thinking," says Ronald Herning, the Johns Hopkins physician who conducted the study. "My advice would be to abstain from using the drug."[23]

Changes in the Body

While the brain changes over time, the body does as well. Most illicit drugs contain ingredients that affect other parts of the body, in both the long and short term. For example, a short-term effect of the hallucinogenic drug phencyclidine (PCP) is a rise in the user's body temperature. That condition often prompts PCP users to strip off their clothes—some have been arrested by police as they wandered naked and disoriented through the streets. In the long term, PCP users have suffered memory loss, speech difficulties, weight loss, reduced blood pressure, respiratory problems, and kidney failure.

Other drugs also attack the kidneys as well as other organs. For example, the toxic ingredients of inhalants that break down the myelin surrounding the neurons also go to work on the other parts of the body. Long-term, inhalants can damage the heart, kidneys, and lungs.

The manufacture of methamphetamine requires the use of acids and solvents, which illegal labs obtain from hardware stores and supermarkets. Drain cleaner and paint thinner are common components of crystal meth. When people who use crystal meth ingest those substances, they risk damage to their throats and esophagi, which are irritated by the caustic chemicals. Crystal meth also rots teeth—a condition known as meth mouth. According to Dominic Ippolito, a fomer meth dealer serving a prison term, "The whole meth-mouth thing is true: I saw hundreds and hundreds of guys with no teeth. A lot of them couldn't even chew the prison food."[24]

Meanwhile, recent studies have started comparing the health effects of marijuana with those of tobacco use. For decades, physicians have warned smokers about the cancer-causing ingredients of tobacco products; now, studies are starting to find similarities between tobacco and marijuana. For example, a Johns Hopkins study found that marijuana

A Utah law enforcement officer examines drug-making paraphernalia seized in a drug raid.

may be as addictive as nicotine, meaning that the pot habit may be just as tough to kick as cigarettes. Other studies have looked at the effects of marijuana smoke on the lungs and other organs and have concluded that people who smoke marijuana, even in moderation, have a higher risk of contracting lung cancer than people who smoke a pack of cigarettes a day. A 2008 New Zealand study found that there are twice as many harmful chemicals in marijuana smoke as there are in cigarette smoke. Indeed, as hazardous as cigarettes may be to human health, at least the filters provided by the cigarette manufacturers sift out some of the cancer-causing chemicals. Marijuana smokers do not use filters, however; pot is typically smoked unfiltered in a pipe or in a homemade cigarette known as a joint.

Moreover, in filtered cigarettes the harmful toxins in tobacco typically accumulate at the end of the cigarette. Many smokers stub out their butts and do not ingest the most concentrated quantities of cigarette tar. In contrast, marijuana smokers burn it all. Once they cannot physically hold the joint in their fingers, they will use metal clips to smoke what is left of the pot. "Cannabis smokers end up with five times more carbon monoxide in their bloodstream (than tobacco smokers)," says

Unlike marijuana smokers, cigarette smokers stub out their butts, thus taking in less carbon monoxide.

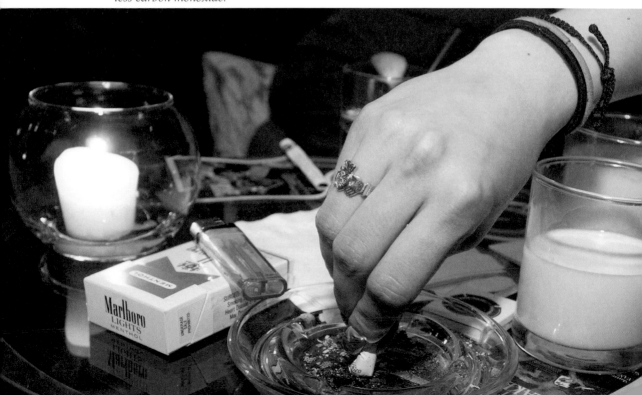

Richard Beasley, director of the study at the Medical Research Institute of New Zealand. "In the near future we may see an epidemic of lung cancers connected with [marijuana]. And the future risk probably applies to many other countries, where increasing use of cannabis among young adults and adolescents is becoming a major public health problem."[25]

Other drugs are no less serious. People who take frequent doses of ecstasy develop motor impairment. They start stumbling or bumping into things even when they are not high. Eventually the effects of long-term ecstasy use can lead to Parkinson's disease—a permanent disorder caused by a shortage of dopamine in the brain. People who are afflicted with Parkinson's disease suffer from tremors. Some have difficulty walking, using their hands, speaking, and thinking clearly.

Ecstasy is also known to affect a user's mental health. Many long-term users of MDMA have been known to suffer depression. Depression is a mental illness characterized by feelings of sadness, hopelessness, and inadequacy. Many people who suffer from depression are unable to get out of bed in the morning. They have little energy to carry out normal functions, such as working, studying, or enjoying themselves in leisure activities. Gordon recalls suffering from depression for months during her ecstasy addiction, finally emerging from mental illness through psychiatric treatment. Of her bout with depression, she states:

> Positive was now negative. I was afraid of happiness. The reason for this curious perception came back to ecstasy. Its highs and lows, during my first euphoric trip and this depression, were freakishly identical in content and structure. The e-world worshipped certain values as godly: love, childhood, grinning, breathing deeply, nature, plastic, grace, excitement, heat, sparkly bright colors, the pleasure of saying "I am happy." Those "godly" values were stamped forever on my mind in my first few experiences with ecstasy. Yet depression saw those values in a different light. I had no chemical capacity to process pleasure. All positive emotion was filtered through a pain so bad I retched with fear of it.[26]

"A Film of Pain"

"The depression was physiological. For the first few days I had thought it was a physical ailment, so forceful was the panic in my heart. . . . I seemed to be enclosed within a film of pain that I felt in my heart and my head and saw all around me."

Olivia Gordon, an ecstasy user and author. Olivia Gordon, *The Agony of Ecstasy*. London: Continuum, 2004, p. 93.

Of course, as newspaper headlines frequently report, the most serious danger of drug abuse is through overdose. Hendrix, the rock guitarist, overdosed by washing down nine sleeping pills with a glass of wine. He fell into such a deep stupor that he was never aware his stomach had rejected the pills, causing him to vomit and drown. Another rock star from the era, Doors singer Jim Morrison, died of a heart attack and internal bleeding after ingesting heroin by inhaling it through his nose. In 1986 University of Maryland basketball star Len Bias celebrated his selection in the NBA draft by ingesting a large quantity of cocaine. The drug stopped his heart, and Bias—a young man at the peak of his athletic ability—died of cardiac arrest. Eleven years later, comedian Chris Farley was found dead; he died after overdosing on a speedball—a concoction of heroin and cocaine. Ironically, Farley, a star on television's *Saturday Night Live*, was regarded as the comedic successor to another *Saturday Night Live* alumnus, John Belushi. In 1982 Belushi died of an overdose after a friend injected him with a speedball.

Steroids and human growth hormone (HGH) have also been responsible for causing fatalities, but the effects of performance-enhancing drugs typically take their toll over a period of several years. Performance-enhancing drugs do not provide their users with narcotic-like highs; rather, they help build up muscle mass, which can enhance strength, athletic performance, and endurance. Once in the body, steroids and HGH are converted to the male hormone testosterone, which helps the body convert protein into muscle mass. Steroids and similar drugs do have benefits, though. Doctors prescribe them to patients whose bodies do not produce testosterone on their own, a condition that could lead to stunted growth or delayed puberty. Also, people who suffer from devastating diseases, such as AIDS, often lose muscle mass as a result of their illnesses. Steroids help them recover their strength.

However, steroids can also be dangerous—particularly in the doses consumed by athletes. Typically, athletes who inject themselves with steroids take massive doses so that they will have deep reservoirs of strength on which to draw for the purposes of competition. Steroids can start showing results within weeks, but the side effects also start showing themselves as well. Among the side effects of steroid use are bloating, weight gain, blood-clotting disorders, liver damage, premature heart attacks, stroke, weak tendons, high blood pressure, acne, kidney ailments, cancer, and personality disorders. Steroid takers have been known to experience wide mood swings, known as "roid rage." Two well-known athletes, football player Lyle Alzado and baseball star Ken Caminiti, admitted to long-term steroid use before they died—Alzado of brain cancer, Caminiti of a sudden heart attack. At the times of their deaths, Alzado was forty-three and Caminiti was forty-one.

Steroids come in many different forms and strengths. While they can influence athletic performance and the recuperation of muscles after hard exercise, they have dangerous side effects.

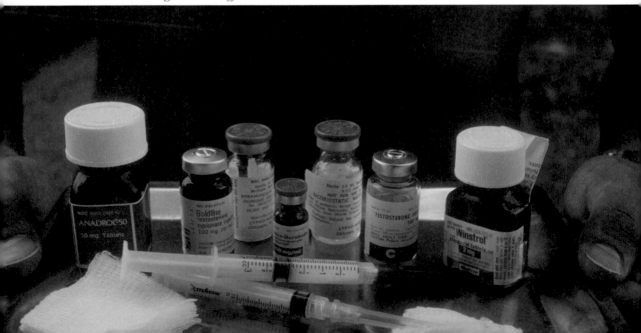

Fearless and Aggressive

In some cases, it is not the drug itself but the method of ingesting the drug that endangers health. Users of heroin and other drugs injected with needles risk contracting hepatitis C, a potentially fatal disease of the liver spread through unclean needles. Even milder diseases, such as mononucleosis, can be spread by sharing drugs. The saliva of an infected mono patient found on the end of a marijuana cigarette can be ingested by someone else who shares the joint.

Sometimes users endanger themselves or others because drugs detract from their coordination or ability to make logical decisions. Certainly, drug abuse has joined alcohol abuse as a significant cause of many automobile accidents over the years. When it comes to this type of danger, some drugs are worse than others. PCP makes users fearless and aggressive and desensitizes them to pain. Many PCP addicts have injured themselves by crashing through windows or by trying to punch their way through walls. In many cases, they do not even know they have hurt themselves. In 1988 James Brown, the late soul singer, led police on a high-speed chase through parts of Georgia and South Carolina before finally crashing his pickup truck. When police pulled the singer out of the wreck, they discovered he was high on PCP. He later served two years in prison.

Profound Consequences

There is no question that drug abuse affects virtually every cell and organ in the body. The marijuana smoker may not realize it, but the brief moments of euphoria he or she feels after drawing on a joint could lead to long-term memory loss, cancer, and other ills. The club-drug user feels a rush of pleasure unlike any he or she has felt before, but those brief moments of euphoria can lead to years of mental illness and even Parkinson's disease. Heroin and crystal meth users seek euphoric highs, but in return they may contract life-threatening illnesses such as AIDS and hepatitis.

Young people who are new to drug abuse are not immune to these dangers. In fact, according to the National Institute on Drug Abuse, a teenager who begins abusing drugs faces a higher risk of addiction—and its subsequent dangers—than others

A New Strain of AIDS

Gay men have always been highly susceptible to contracting acquired immune deficiency syndrome (AIDS). In recent years, a new epidemic of AIDS has surfaced among gay men who use crystal meth. Methamphetamine prompts its users to drop their inhibitions; among some gays, that often means a propensity for engaging in unprotected sex.

According to a 2005 study by the Los Angeles Lesbian and Gay Center, nearly one in three gay men in Los Angeles who have tested positive for AIDS have used crystal meth. Physicians in other cities have seen similar trends in the gay community. A 2003 study by the New York City Health Department found more than half the gay men in the city who engaged in sex with multiple partners had contracted AIDS, which officials attributed to unprotected sex prompted by meth use.

Doctors have determined that a new strain of AIDS circulating in the gay community is particularly virulent: The virus does not respond to drugs that are effective in treating other strains of the disease. Patrick McGovern, executive director of the Harlem United Community AIDS Center in New York, says, "In the past twelve or fifteen months, we've seen a huge increase in meth use among people that are newly tested [for AIDS]. People become hypersexual when they're using crystal."

Quoted in Richard Pérez-Peña and Marc Santora, "AIDS Report Brings Alarm, Not Surprise," *New York Times*, February 13, 2005, p. I-1.

who are older. During adolescence, the brain is still growing and developing. By using drugs in adolescence, the young drug abuser may hard-wire addiction into his or her brain, making it a function of the way he or she thinks. According to *The Science of Addiction*:

> One of the brain areas still maturing during adolescence is the prefrontal cortex—the part of the brain that enables us to assess situations, make sound decisions, and keep our emotions and desires under control. The fact that this critical part of an adolescent's brain is still a work-in-progress puts them at increased risk for poor decisions (such as trying drugs or continued abuse). Thus, introducing drugs while the brain is still developing may have profound and long-lasting consequences.[27]

How Drug Abuse Affects Society

Drug abuse has a profound impact on virtually every segment of American society. According to the National Institute on Drug Abuse, 31 percent of homeless people in America suffer from either a drug or alcohol addiction. Likewise, some 60 percent of inmates in federal prisons have been convicted of crimes related to drugs. Children born to mothers who abused drugs are more likely to be developmentally disabled than others, forcing taxpayers to pick up the costs for their special education needs. In the workplace, heavy drug users frequently miss work, placing a burden on their employers as well as their coworkers, who are forced to cover for them. As many as 80 percent of children who are victims of abuse live in homes where parents are known to consume alcohol and drugs. "Directly or indirectly," says a National Institute on Drug Abuse report, "every community is affected by drug abuse and addiction, as is every family. Drugs take a tremendous toll on our society at many levels."[28]

One of the most devastating impacts of drug abuse is the way it tears apart families. As a father falls deeper and deeper into the drug culture, his connection to his family grows less and less. He no longer comes home at night. He misses soccer games and school recitals. He may lose his job, denying his family food and shelter. The case of Terry Silvers provides a typical example of how a hardworking and loving father sacrificed it all for drugs. Silvers had a good job in a Georgia carpet mill. One day he stopped in a bar after work with some friends. Silvers had too much to drink and worried about driving home. To help him wake up, a friend offered Silvers some crystal meth. He tried the drug—and then came back for more. Within months, Silvers cared for nothing other than finding more meth. He quit his job, stopped eating regularly, and lost forty pounds. He also started making methamphetamine. When Silvers flew into a drug frenzy and beat up his wife, Lisa, police were summoned. Silvers was incarcerated and charged with operating a meth lab. Lisa Silvers says, "I think meth is one of the plagues the Bible talks about."[29]

FEELING ALONE

"You feel alone in this, ashamed, like no other family is affected by this, but we learned that's just not true in this county. So many families like ours are going through the same thing."

Richard Gauthier of Simi Valley, California, whose son, Chad, was addicted to methamphetamine. Quoted in Tamara Koehler, "Teens and Their Families Struggle to Overcome Meth's Grip," *Ventura County Star*, October 21, 2007. www.venturacountystar.com/news/2007/oct/21/teens-families-struggle-with-meth.

The Reid Family Crisis

The Silvers family is not unique. Across America, families are constantly being devastated by drug addiction. Sometimes it happens to the family that friends and others would least suspect of being affected by drug abuse—a family like the Reids.

In 2007 the sons of Philadelphia Eagles coach Andy Reid were arrested on drug-related charges in separate incidents. As the story unfolded, it became apparent that Britt and Garrett Reid had both suffered from long-term addictions. For months, the stories of the two Reid sons dominated the headlines, sports talk shows, and other media in Philadelphia as well as the rest of the country. Fans debated whether the Reid sons would be imprisoned or whether the judge would treat them with leniency as a favor to their famous father. Fans also wondered what effect the arrests would have on the team.

The incidents erupted on January 30, 2007, when police responded to a road-rage case on a suburban Philadelphia street in which Britt Reid, twenty-two, was alleged to have pointed a gun at another driver. Inside Britt's car, police found a .45-caliber pistol; a shotgun; ammunition; and quantities of cocaine, marijuana, and prescription painkillers. Later that day police pursued a car driving at a high rate of speed. The pursuit ended in a crash that injured another driver. When police finally caught up with the car they had been chasing, they found Britt's twenty-four-year-old brother, Garrett, at the wheel. Inside Garrett's car, police found quantities of heroin, pills, and a scale for weighing drugs.

Garrett (bottom left) and Britt Reid, sons of Philadelphia Eagles coach Andy Reid (top) were convicted of drug use.

That day, Garrett tested positive for heroin and was charged with driving under the influence.

Both of the coach's sons would get into trouble again. While awaiting trial on bail, Britt used drugs and crashed his car in the parking lot of a sporting goods store. Meanwhile, Garrett was charged with attempting to smuggle drugs into prison while awaiting trial. After his second arrest, Garrett resolved to stay clean. "I'm at the point in my life where I have already made the decision that I don't want to die doing drugs," Garrett told his probation officer. "I don't want to be that kid who was the son of the head coach of the Eagles, who was spoiled and on drugs and OD'd [overdosed] and just faded into oblivion."[30]

TAKING ACCOUNTABILITY

"I have some real difficulty with the structure in which these two boys live. What is the supervision? You've got to take accountability for what goes on in the house."

Judge Steven O'Neill, who criticized Philadelphia Eagles coach Andy Reid and his wife, Tammy, after learning that drugs and guns were found in the Reid home. Quoted in Wendy Ruderman, "Reid Sons Are Sent to Jail," *Philadelphia Daily News*, November 2, 2007. www. philly.com/dailynews/top_story/20071102_REID_SONS_ARE_SENT_TO_JAIL.html.

As for whether the judge would show leniency to the Reid family, that matter was settled when Britt and Garrett each received jail sentences of up to two years. In fact, Judge Steven O'Neill was particularly harsh on the Reid family, believing the lack of parental authority in the home led to the coach's sons becoming addicted to drugs. The judge suggested that the Reid home may not be the best place for Garrett and Britt once they are released from prison. "This is a family in crisis," O'Neill said in court. "There isn't any structure there that this court can depend on."[31]

Throughout the months that their cases were pending, Andy Reid found himself under tremendous pressure to publicly discuss the addictions of his two sons. He steadfastly refused, seeking to maintain his family's privacy. At one point during the year, Reid took a leave of absence from the team so he could devote himself full time to his family. There was even much talk during the season that Reid would resign as coach. "Reid and his family have been though a lot," wrote *Washington Post* sports columnist Mark Maske at the time. "It would only be natural and human for him to give serious thought to doing something less demanding and time-consuming than coaching an NFL team, and putting his focus on other areas of his life."[32]

Finally, after Britt and Garrett were sentenced, Reid and his wife, Tammy, gave an interview to a magazine reporter. The Reids acknowledged that their sons had gotten into drugs years before, and that they found themselves powerless to wean them away from their addictions. "You have no idea, as parents you have no idea what's right and what's wrong, what's going to work and what's not going to work," Tammy Reid said. "And so you take a stab at it, you talk to psychologists and psychiatrists and friends who have been through it, anybody, to come up with a solution, what you think is best, and it doesn't always work."[33]

Drugs in the Workplace

The Silvers and Reid families paid high prices for the drug addictions of Terry Silvers and Britt and Garrett Reid, but in reality everyone pays the cost of addiction. In 2002 a report by the White House Office of National Drug Control Policy suggested that drug abuse places an annual burden of $181 billion on the economy. According to the report, "This value represents both the use of resources to address health and crime consequences as well as the loss of potential productivity from disability, death and withdrawal from the legitimate workforce."[34] Moreover, the report said the economic burden of drug abuse has been rising at a rate of about 5 percent a year.

According to the Office of National Drug Control Policy, the largest share of that $181 billion, about $128 billion, represents the cost of lost productivity—the wasted time at work that drug users cause because they do not perform at the best of their abilities or they simply miss work. A report by the agency explains that "productivity losses represent work in the labor market and in household production that was never performed, but could reasonably be expected to be performed absent the impact of drug abuse."[35]

The Story of Diane Linkletter

One of the first family tragedies to be linked to drug abuse revolved around the family of Art Linkletter, the popular host of the 1950s and 1960s daytime television talk show *House Party*. In 1969 Linkletter's twenty-year-old daughter, Diane, committed suicide, leaping to her death from a sixth-floor window.

Diane had been a user of LSD, which her father blamed for her death. However, an investigation indicated that there were no drugs in Diane's body and that she had not used LSD for a year before her death. Evidently, she was depressed and despondent—factors that are at the root of many suicides. Still, her father steadfastly blamed her drug abuse and used his celebrity status to warn parents of the dangers of drug addiction.

The urban legend that Diane Linkletter had used LSD at the time of her death was helped along by a quickie film produced in 1970 by independent film director John Waters. Titled *The Diane Linkletter Story*, the film portrays the television host's daughter as hopelessly addicted to marijuana and psychedelic drugs. Despite the thin evidence that LSD caused Diane Linkletter's death, the public still felt much empathy for her father and agreed with the notion that drugs caused Diane to take her own life.

Art Linkletter is pictured with son Jack and daughter Diane. Linkletter blamed Diane's suicide on her drug use.

There is no question that employees who abuse drugs do not make very good workers. A 1999 study by the U.S. Substance Abuse and Mental Health Services Administration (SAMHSA) found that drug-abusing workers typically miss at least one day of work a month and are more likely to change jobs often. The SAMHSA said a study of U.S. Postal Service employees found that 66 percent of employees who admit to regular drug abuse are likely to be frequently absent from their jobs. In addition, the dismissal rate among such employees is high: 77 percent of postal workers who admit to drug abuse lose their jobs. The SAMHSA study also looked at drug use among railroad employees and found that in one-third of all accidents that occur on the railways, a key employee involved in the accident was abusing either drugs or alcohol.

Many employers are on the lookout for workers who may be abusing drugs as well as other substances—and not necessarily to fire them. Many companies provide substance abuse programs that make counseling and rehabilitation available to workers who come forward and admit their addictions. In most cases, though, it is largely up to the employee to own up to an addiction and seek help. Terry Silvers's company had a substance abuse program. Lisa Silvers urged her husband to enroll in the program, but he refused to acknowledge his addiction and instead quit the company and went into the meth business.

Even though many companies try to provide drug intervention to addicted employees, drug abuse at the workplace continues to cost the economy billions of dollars each year, although many employers require prospective employees to submit to drug tests as a condition for employment. Typically, job applicants are asked to provide urine samples, which are then analyzed by drug-testing laboratories. In most cases, though, once the employees start work they are no longer required to submit to additional drug tests. There are exceptions to that practice, particularly in professional sports.

The Saga of Ricky Williams

Most professional sports leagues require players to undergo random drug tests throughout the season, and those drug tests have often resulted in players facing fines, suspensions, and even banishment from their leagues. There is no question that drug abuse has cut short many professional sports careers, costing highly skilled athletes millions of dollars in salary. Teams that come to rely on their biggest stars find themselves scrambling to replace those players. In some cases, it may take a team years to recover from losing a key player to drugs. Of course, the biggest losers are the fans who miss out on the excitement of watching their favorite players.

The case of Ricky Williams serves as a prime example of an athlete whose drug abuse all but ruined his career as well as the fortunes of his team. In 1998 the running back from the University of Texas won the Heisman Trophy as the top college football player of the year. A few months later he was selected as one of the top picks in the NFL draft. Despite some good early seasons, Williams's NFL career has been hampered by his addiction to marijuana. Williams has flunked five drug tests, a circumstance that has caused him to serve long suspensions. He even retired from the game at one point to pursue a career in natural medicine and be able to smoke pot without the constant harassment of NFL officials. During his retirement in 2004, a reporter asked

Miami Dolphins player Ricky Williams served long suspensions from the NFL after failing drug tests for marijuana. He later quit the NFL in order to smoke marijuana without harassment.

Williams whether he continued to use marijuana. He answered, "Well, I'm not in the NFL so what does it matter?"[36]

A short time later, Williams reconsidered and applied for reinstatement to the NFL. He was accepted back but was forced to serve suspensions for failing drug tests. Now in his thirties—an advanced age for an NFL running back—Williams has played in only a handful of games in the past few years. Meanwhile, his team, the Miami Dolphins, has struggled to find a player of Williams's caliber to replace him in the backfield—a circumstance that helped Miami finish 2007 with a dismal record of only one win and fifteen losses, one of the worst records compiled by an NFL team in years. Williams hopes to continue his comeback, but there is no question that Williams, his team, and his fans have suffered because of his drug abuse, which is responsible for holding back what could have been an incandescent career on the field.

Steroids in Sports

Another form of drug abuse that has rocked sports in recent years is the abuse of illegal performance-enhancing substances, such as steroids and HGH. The substances can help weightlifters lift heavier weights, track stars run faster, football linemen block more effectively, and baseball players hit balls farther or throw pitches harder. There is no question that using steroids or HGH is cheating. All professional and college leagues have outlawed the use of performance-enhancing drugs. Still, athletes find a way to skirt the rules and inject themselves with steroids, which has cast a shadow over professional sports as fans question whether everyone plays by the same rules.

TELLING THE TRUTH

"When I told Senator Mitchell that I injected Roger Clemens with performance-enhancing drugs, I told the truth. I told the truth about steroids and human growth hormone. I injected those drugs into the body of Roger Clemens at his direction."

Brian McNamee, former trainer for Roger Clemens. Quoted in David Aldridge, "Clemens and Steroids: Capitol Hardball," *Philadelphia Inquirer*, February 14, 2008, p. A-20.

The Mitchell Report

Even though Major League Baseball instituted a drug-testing program in 2003, rumors of use of performance-enhancing drugs in baseball persisted, particularly after a 2005 U.S. House hearing in which former slugger Jose Canseco charged that use of steroids and human growth hormone (HGH) are widespread in the sport.

George Mitchell testifies at a congressional hearing about his findings of rampant drug use in professional baseball.

In 2006 Major League Baseball officials retained George Mitchell, a former U.S. senator, to investigate use of performance-enhancing drugs by players.

Mitchell released his 409-page report in December 2007, naming eighty-six players—including some of the sport's biggest stars—as users of steroids and HGH. After release of the report, officials pledged to institute stricter testing procedures and clean up the sport. As for the players named in the report, Mitchell did not recommend punishment. It soon became clear, however, that many of the stars would be made to pay a steep price, such as banishment from the Baseball Hall of Fame. According to the Mitchell report, "The illegal use of performance-enhancing substances poses a serious threat to the integrity of the game. Widespread use by players of such substances unfairly disadvantages the honest athletes who refuse to use them and raises questions about the validity of baseball records."

Quoted in CBS News, "Mitchell Report Names Baseball Steroid Users," December 13, 2007. http://cbs2chicago.com/national/Mitchell.report.baseball.2.609138.html.

The steroid scandal has also led to criminal charges filed against baseball's most acclaimed star, career home-run record holder Barry Bonds. The slugger is alleged to have used performance-enhancing drugs for many years and to have lied to investigators about how he obtained the substances. A report issued in 2007 by former U.S. senator George Mitchell for Major League Baseball found rampant use of steroids in professional baseball. The report named some of the game's biggest stars as habitual steroid users, including seven-time Cy Young Award–winning pitcher Roger Clemens. Meanwhile, in track and field, sprinter Marion Jones was sentenced in 2008 to six months in prison and must return her gold medals from the 2000 Olympic Games after lying to investigators about how she obtained performance-enhancing drugs. In sentencing the track star to a prison term, Judge Kenneth Karas said, "Athletes in society have an elevated status, they entertain, they inspire, and perhaps, most important, they serve as role models."[37]

Steroid Use Denied

"I have never taken steroids or HGH. No matter what we discuss here today, I am never going to have my name restored."

Pitcher Roger Clemens, testifying in 2008 before a U.S. House committee investigating steroid use in Major League Baseball. Quoted in David Aldridge, "Clemens and Steroids: Capitol Hardball," *Philadelphia Inquirer*, February 14, 2008, p. A-1.

The Costs of Health Care

The abuse of steroids and other illegal drugs frequently leads to long-term health consequences, which was also cited in the Office of National Drug Control Policy's report on the economic impact of drugs on society. Each year money must be spent on the hospitalization and rehabilitation of drug abusers who overdose. It also goes into the cost of caring for babies who are born with birth defects because their mothers abused drugs during pregnancy. Drug abusers who use unclean needles often spread such diseases as hepatitis and AIDS; their care is often long and expensive. Finally, innocent people are often affected by drug abusers. They may be the victims of auto accidents caused by drivers who are under the influence of drugs, or they may be people who were assaulted by drug abusers in need of money to buy narcotics. As these various costs rise, so does the cost of health insurance, which pays most of the medical bills in the American economy. That means the cost of health insurance continues to rise, which impacts companies and their workers, who typically share in the cost of health insurance, as well as individuals who may pay for insurance on their own. According to the Office of National Drug Control Policy, when it is all added up, drug abuse contributes $15 billion a year to the cost of health care in America.

There are many other costs as well, including the cost of investigating, prosecuting, and imprisoning drug dealers; the cost of running treatment and rehabilitation centers; and the cost to the environment that occurs when toxic residue from illegal labs is dumped into rivers or streams. Such costs total about $38 billion a year. "Drugs are a direct threat to the economic security of the United States," says John P. Walters, director of the Office of National Drug Control Policy. "Drug use results in lower productivity, more workplace accidents, and higher health care costs. . . . When we talk about the toll that drugs take on our country—especially on our young people—we usually point to the human costs: lives ruined, potential extinguished, and dreams derailed."[38]

420 Rallies

Certainly, many young people do face the likelihood that their dreams will be derailed due to their addiction to drugs. Indeed, it seems that in every middle school and high school and on every college campus, everyone seems to know the drug users. They are the students who are absent a lot and who never seem to have their homework assignments finished on time. These students consistently get low grades, and in many cases, they ultimately drop out of school. According to SAMHSA, the illegal drug abuse rate among high school dropouts is 22 percent.

It is impossible to know when the first teenager smoked the first joint in high school, but the practice does have something of a recorded history. In 1971 a group of five students gathered to smoke marijuana every day at 4:20 P.M. at the foot of the statue of Louis Pasteur on the grounds of San Rafael High School in California. Soon, the term *420* became a codeword in the drug culture. (It is also a codeword in the law enforcement community. In some police departments, when an officer announces a "420" over the police radio, it means he or she is investigating a case related to marijuana.)

The Second Annual Millennium Marijuana March is held in Seattle, Washington. Such marches are traditionally held on April 20th.

Over the years, 420 has become an unofficial holiday for marijuana smokers. Students on many college campuses stage 420 rallies on April 20 each year to support marijuana smoking. One school where students often stage 420 rallies is the University of California at Santa Cruz, which *Rolling Stone* magazine chronicled in a 2004 story titled "The Most Stoned Kids on the Most Stoned Day on the Most Stoned Campus on Earth."

Rolling Stone reported on the activities on that day of two students, named Moppy and Molly, as they smoked pot and prepared for the 420 rally. But as the story indicates, Molly and Moppy do not have to wait for April 20 to get high. Each student claimed to smoke a prodigious amount of marijuana every day. "We have the best weed in the world in Santa Cruz,"[39] said Molly.

As a result, Molly has failed a lot of classes. As for Moppy, he does get good grades but admits to going to classes stoned. Both students failed to graduate on time and had to enroll in school for an extra semester. Molly seems to know, though, that her addiction now controls her life. In an essay for a college class, Molly wrote,

> I wake up in the morning when my dreams run out to find another sad day awaiting me. I miss the days when I was young and every moment was magical. Had my spirit become so sick of me, as to run away like this? I am mostly scared at this point. I am scared of growing up and I am scared of myself, because I know that I have almost lost control.[40]

Drug abuse can sweep through an entire college campus, as it has at the University of California at Santa Cruz. Certainly, drug abuse can affect individual families like the Silverses. The addictions of Britt and Garrett Reid caught the attention of hundreds of thousands of people in Philadelphia as an entire city followed the tragic story that engulfed the family of a popular football coach. And as the White House Office of National Drug Control Policy study proves, drug abuse has a definite impact on the American economy, costing billions of dollars a year. As for the cost in human suffering, that may be incalculable.

CHAPTER 4

THE WAR ON DRUGS

The U.S. Drug Enforcement Administration (DEA) regularly reports its achievements when it breaks up major narcotics rings. In 2007, for example, the DEA busted a Texas-based ring responsible for importing some 2.7 tons (2.5t) of cocaine and 33 tons (30t) of marijuana into the United States from Mexico. In another operation, DEA agents working with the U.S. Coast Guard seized a ship off the coast of Panama that was carrying nearly 21.5 tons (19.5t) of cocaine. Clearly, the ship was heading for the United States when it was boarded by authorities. In another 2007 case, DEA agents arrested some four hundred people nationwide who were alleged to have been distributing cocaine and marijuana smuggled into the United States by a single Mexican drug lord, Victor Emilio Cazares-Gastellum. DEA administrator Karen Tandy states, "The Cazares-Gastellum drug empire that rose to such heights of power in only two years fell today at the hands of DEA and our partners."[41]

Indeed, the statistics compiled by law enforcement agencies are staggering. According to an analysis by *Rolling Stone* magazine, nearly five hundred thousand Americans were behind bars on drug offenses in 2003. During the past thirty-five years, the federal, state, and local governments in America have spent some $500 billion to stem the flow of drugs into the country.

But has it worked? DEA agents and other officials are quick to concede that as soon as one drug kingpin is put behind bars, another quickly takes his place. "We've been working in Colombia for thirty years, and we don't have a hell of a lot to show for it," says

A U.S. Coast Guard officer guards 21.4 tons (19.4t) of cocaine confiscated from a cargo ship.

Myles Frechette, a former U.S. ambassador to Colombia. "This is like a cancer. Every year the lesion, if you took a snapshot, would look bigger."[42]

Controlled Substances

Although America's war on drugs can be traced back to the appointment of Harry Anslinger as head of the Federal Bureau of Narcotics in 1932, there were few resources and little organization devoted to the effort until 1968, when President Lyndon B. Johnson consolidated a number of federal law enforcement agencies into the Bureau of Narcotics and Dangerous Drugs in the U.S. Justice Department. In 1970 Congress passed the landmark U.S. Controlled Substances Act, which defined five classes of drugs according to their potential for abuse as well as their use for legitimate medicinal purposes. Whereas schedule I drugs were defined as most likely to be abused and least likely to have use as legitimate medications, schedule V drugs were defined as those least likely to be abused with the most potential for legitimate medicinal purposes. Marijuana, for example, was designated as a schedule I drug, meaning it has a high potential for abuse and has no legitimate medicinal use. Since then, state governments have based their laws regulating drug use and setting penalties for possession and distribution of drugs based on the schedules of drugs established in 1970. (Over the years, other drugs have been added to the list of controlled substances.)

TOUGH TALK

"One of the things that I think is a problem is that we are not doing enough that is morally proportional to the nature of the offense. . . . Ask most Americans if they saw somebody out on the streets selling drugs to their kid what they would feel morally justifiable in doing—tear them limb from limb."

William Bennett, former director of the White House Office of National Drug Control Policy. Quoted in Jodi Dean, ed., *Cultural Studies and Political Theory*. Ithaca, NY: Cornell University Press, 2000, p. 38.

By then, a number of scientific studies had been issued chronicling the dangers of addiction and linking drug abuse with crime. President Richard M. Nixon declared drug abuse "public enemy number one in the United States"[43] and ordered a number of measures to crack down on traffickers. Some of the measures implemented during the Nixon administration, such as Operation Intercept, were quickly discarded. Under Operation Intercept, U.S. customs agents attempted to search every vehicle entering the United States along the Mexican border. It was supposed to take just three minutes to search each vehicle, but after two weeks the program was shelved. Operation Intercept caused huge backups

Breaking the French Connection

The first big victory scored by police in the drug war occurred in 1962, when police in New York City broke up what was known as the French Connection—the importation of massive amounts of heroin to the United States from France. For decades, opium grown in Turkey was ferried to Marseilles, a Mediterranean seaport city in France, where underworld traffickers converted it to heroin. From Marseilles, the gangsters shipped the heroin to America, mostly hiding it in legitimate cargo aboard ships.

The case was cracked by two New York City detectives, Eddie Egan and Sonny Grasso, whose dogged investigation led them to suspect a French television star, Jacques Angelvin, of smuggling heroin in a car he had transported to America aboard a ship. After searching the car, Egan and Grasso found a secret compartment containing more than 100 pounds (45kg) of pure heroin. The drugs had a street value at the time of more than $25 million. Finding the drugs in Angelvin's car helped Egan and Grasso build a case against four other suspects, eventually leading them to a New York City home where they found another 88 pounds (40kg) of heroin, ready for distribution to street dealers.

at the border crossings, causing people to wait hours before they could cross into the United States. In the meantime, the economies of the border states suffered because Mexican laborers refused to cross into the United States for their jobs. Other commerce suffered as well. Operation Intercept did temporarily slow the flow of marijuana into the country, but drug abuse experts noticed that users turned to other, more readily available substances, particularly LSD, until the supply of pot returned to pre–Operation Intercept levels.

Other initiatives during the Nixon administration, such as establishment of the Drug Enforcement Administration in 1973, have paid much higher dividends. The DEA was formed with an eye toward making the war on drugs an international effort. To create the organization, agents were drawn from the Bureau of Narcotics and Dangerous Drugs as well as the U.S. Customs Service and Central Intelligence Agency (CIA). The addition of the customs and CIA agents into the DEA indicated a willingness by federal officials to root out traffickers in Latin America, Asia, and other places that served as the sources of the drugs imported into America.

Colombian Cartels

The DEA had good reason to turn its attention to the Latin American countries. It was becoming more and more obvious that Colombia and other countries in South and Central America were serving as prime exporting centers for illegal drugs. Indeed, in the remote mountains of Colombia, farmers grew coca, the source of the main ingredient of cocaine, virtually unmolested by police. Meanwhile, secret labs hidden deep in the Colombian jungles processed the coca into cocaine. It was all being produced under the guidance of illegal drug cartels. And there was no question that the cartels were ruthless and violent.

In 1975 police seized 1,300 pounds (600kg) of cocaine from a small airplane at the airport in Cali, Colombia. A few days later, forty people were found murdered in the nearby city of Medellín. Investigators speculated they were low-level members of the ring who paid the ultimate price for letting the drugs fall into the hands of the police.

By the 1980s, the Colombian drug cartels had grown increasingly bold. They no longer carried out the pretense of operating in secret. Some of the drug kingpins built lavish mansions, employed private armies, and were clearly operating with the knowledge of government officials and police who were on their payrolls. One Colombian kingpin, Carlos Lehder, bought most of the tiny island of Norman's Cay in the Bahamas, just 200 miles (322km) from Florida. From the island, Lehder openly dispatched small planes to America, where they landed on remote airstrips and unloaded their cargoes of cocaine. In 1982, under pressure from the U.S. government, authorities in the Bahamas closed down the operation and kicked Lehder off the island.

Back in Colombia, American officials pressured the government to arrest cartel leaders and extradite them to United States, where they had been indicted on drug charges. After several reformers in Colombia were assassinated by the cartels, Colombian police mounted an offensive against the drug kingpins, killing some in violent clashes and jailing others. In 1993 one of the top Colombian drug kingpins, Pablo Escobar, was killed in a shoot-out with Colombian police.

Meanwhile, efforts in other Latin American countries were also starting to show results. In 1988 U.S. prosecutors indicted Panamanian president Manuel Noriega, accused of laundering drug money and providing Colombian kingpins with safe havens in his country, where they had established laboratories. A year later

Shipping Drugs by Submersibles

American drug agents are used to searching the skies for small airplanes ferrying drugs into the United States. Now, they find themselves looking beneath the waves as well.

In recent years, U.S. Coast Guard patrols have captured thirteen crudely built submersible vessels filled with cargoes of cocaine. The boats are not truly submarines—they cannot dive beneath the surface. Rather, they travel at a depth

Columbian police and navy officers investigate a submersible that was being built by drug lords. When finished, the boat could have held 200 tons of cocaine.

just below the surface of the water, with only their cockpits and exhaust pipes visible above the sea. Still, the submersibles can travel virtually in secret to American waters.

The boats are built in makeshift factories hidden deep in the Colombian jungles. It is estimated that each boat takes about a year to construct and costs about $2 million. Each boat has the capability of carrying 10 tons (9.1t) of cocaine, which can fetch some $200 million in profits in America.

Coast Guard and Colombian navy officials believe many boats are still in operation. Colombian navy captain Gustavo Angel says, "What's most striking is the logistical capacity of these criminals to take all this material into the jungle, including heavy equipment like propulsion gear and generators."

Quoted in Juan Forero, "Underground Drug Trade Is Going Underwater, Too," *Philadelphia Inquirer,* February 10, 2008, p. A-9.

American troops invaded Panama, where they captured Noriega and brought him back to Florida. Noriega was tried, convicted, and sentenced to forty years in prison. Federal authorities have continued to target countries in Central and South America. In 2000 President Bill Clinton launched Plan Colombia, a program to fund Colombian military initiatives against drug kingpins. Initially budgeted at $1 billion, Plan Colombia has grown into a $5 billion initiative that continues to be funded each year by Congress.

While it would seem that the initiatives against the Colombian cartels, the arrests of high-level traffickers like Noriega, and the implementation of programs such as Plan Colombia would have virtually wiped out the Latin American drug trade, that has not been the case. Despite all those efforts, drugs continue to flow into the United States. According to an analysis by *Rolling Stone*, in 2000 some 242 tons (219.5t) of cocaine were smuggled into the United States through Mexico; five years later, those shipments totaled 397 tons (360t).

SHIPPING CONTAINERS

"Even if somehow we could manage to get the drug trade away from the Mexican border, it will come through Asia next. Instead of fighting a border war, we'll be fighting it in [shipping] containers."

Tony Payan, a political science professor at the University of Texas at El Paso and an expert on drug trafficking. Quoted in Ben Wallace-Wells, "How America Lost the Drug War," *Rolling Stone*, December 13, 2007, p. 117.

Not all drugs find their way into the United States across the Mexican border. Much of the heroin sold in America originates in the opium fields of Thailand and other Asian countries. In Afghanistan the drug trade is believed to be financing the resurgence of the Taliban, the regime that provided shelter for the terrorists who planned and carried out the September 11, 2001, attacks on the World Trade Center and the Pentagon. Meanwhile, many drugs cross the Canadian border. In late 2007 drug agents in Onondaga County, New York, broke up a ring that had smuggled some 6 tons (5.4t) of marijuana into the United States over the Canadian border.

Moreover, not all drugs are imported. Methamphetamine, for example, is mostly manufactured in basement labs found in America. Usually, these labs are not discovered until they accidentally blow up.

Given the huge amount of drugs making their way into the hands of abusers, it seems as though the thirst of Americans for illegal drugs is as strong as ever. According to Lee Brown, the head of the White House Office of National Drug Control Policy under President Clinton:

> When I worked as an undercover narcotics officer, I was living the life of an addict so I could make buys and make busts of the dealers. When you're in that position, you see very quickly that you can't arrest your way out of this. You see the cycle over and over again of people using drugs, getting into trouble, going to prison, getting out, and getting into drugs again.[44]

The Central City Massacre

This nonstop delivery of drugs onto American streets is the top reason for most of the crime committed in America. In 2002 the White House Office of National Drug Control Policy estimated that drug-related crime costs the national economy some $108 billion a year. In fact, the agency reported, some 60 percent of all crime in America is drug related. In addition to crime that is directly related to drugs—such as the manufacture and distribution of illicit drugs or the violence and murder committed by rival drug gangs—other criminal acts often have roots in the drug trade. Thieves steal to feed their drug habits. People who abuse drugs often drive under the influence, causing accidents and injuring or killing innocent people. Sometimes innocent and unsuspecting people are caught in the violent crossfire of drug dealers' gun battles, with tragic results.

In many cases, drug violence can be particularly horrific. In the early morning hours of June 17, 2006, police in New Orleans were called to the intersection of Danneel and Josephine streets in the city's tough Central City neighborhood. When they arrived, police were stunned by what they found: the bodies of five teenagers, all killed in a hail of gunfire. Later that day police arrested nineteen-year-old Michael Anderson and charged him with the murders of the five young people, all between the ages of sixteen and nineteen. According to police, the five victims were sitting in a car when Anderson approached the vehicle, killing the driver first and then opening fire into the car, spraying the interior of the vehicle with some twenty bullets. Police speculated that Anderson killed the youths in a dispute over drug territory. Anderson and some of the boys in the car had long histories of drug abuse and arrests on drug charges.

The fight over control of drug territory is often accompanied by violence. Michael Anderson is arrested after killing five young people also involved in the drug trade.

The prosecution against Anderson hit some roadblocks. After initially charging him with the murders, prosecutors were forced to drop the case because of the reluctance of witnesses to step forward and testify. This is a common occurrence in drug cases because, often, most of the people with knowledge of the case are also in the illegal drug business. As New Orleans defense attorney Dane Ciolino explains, "If you are hanging around selling crack, and the guy gets shot next to you, you are a witness who doesn't want to come forward."[45]

SNITCHES

"[Snitches are] people that are engaged in illegal activities, making a profit from it, and then when it comes time for the curtains to close—you do the crime, you do the time—now no one wants to go to jail. The old lady that lives on the block that [calls] the police because guys are selling drugs in front of her house, she's not a snitch because she is what would be considered a civilian."

Rodney Bethea, a Baltimore, Maryland, man who produced an underground DVD encouraging witnesses to keep their silence. Quoted in Jeremy Kahn, "The Story of a Snitch," *Atlantic*, April 2007, p. 80.

In fact, according to Jimmy Keen, head of the homicide unit for the New Orleans police, prosecutors in the city are able to win convictions in just 30 percent of drug-related killings, mostly because of the reluctance of witnesses to testify. As for the Central City massacre, the public and political leaders placed intense pressure on the police to solve the murders and, eventually, police convinced some key witnesses to testify. The case against Anderson was refiled, and prosecutors announced their intentions to seek the death penalty. "We're happy that Michael Anderson is looking at the death penalty for his actions,"[46] says police superintendent Warren Riley.

The type of violence that occurred in New Orleans is not unusual in the drug culture. Shootings related to drugs occur virtually every day in every large American city. Drug violence happens elsewhere as well, including small towns like Rutland, Vermont. On February 4, 2008, twenty-nine-year-old Carlos Vasquez was shot to death on a Rutland street, the victim of a drug deal gone bad. Soon after the murder, officials of Rutland called on the governor of Vermont to make extra funds available to pay overtime to Rutland police so they could investigate drug dealing in the town. "We could have the best roads and water and sewer infrastructure, but it doesn't mean anything if people are dying in the streets,"[47] says Christopher Louras, mayor of Rutland.

Moving Marijuana Indoors

The drug culture can be found in tough urban neighborhoods like Central City and picturesque small towns like Rutland. It can also be found in rural communities like Kosciusko County, Indiana, where police unearthed a sprawling field of marijuana plants in 2007. The crop covered 20 acres (8.1ha) and included thousands of marijuana plants, some as tall as 7 feet (2.13m). Each day, Kosciusko resident Wellington White rode his horse past the field and never realized a crop of marijuana plants was growing near his home. "There's ten, twenty acres of pot plants here," he told a news reporter. "They're everywhere."[48] When police find marijuana fields, they typically dispose of the plants by tearing them out of the ground, soaking them with diesel fuel or a similar flammable substance, and lighting them on fire.

There is no question that drug producers look for very remote places to grow marijuana. Sometimes they find them in national parks. Some national parks are so big that marijuana growers have found they can raise their crops unmolested by park rangers, hikers, campers, and other visitors. Typically, the growers select the most remote, most inaccessible places in the park to grow marijuana. Still, the police do find ways to make busts in national parks. In 2005 drug agents removed some forty-four thousand marijuana plants from Sequoia National Park in California. "I've had meetings with law enforcement throughout the state, and everybody just sits there with their mouths open," says William Ruzzamenti, a DEA agent who heads a task force that investigates marijuana growing in national parks. "Nobody can believe this has happened on the scale that it has."[49]

In many cases, police have used helicopters and airplanes to provide aerial surveillance to help them find marijuana fields. Such

Marijuana grows in a remote, rural location.

aggressive techniques have prompted many marijuana growers to move their operations indoors. Now, in addition to looking for drugs in rural fields, police must also concentrate on inner-city and suburban neighborhoods, where homes are equipped with "grow rooms." Such rooms, usually located in basements, feature rows and rows of plants growing under high-intensity lights. As such, police must employ infrared tracking devices to help them find sources of the intense heat given off by the lights.

For example, in 2007 police raided an ordinary-looking brick house in Coldwater Creek, Georgia, a suburb of Atlanta. In the basement, they found 680 marijuana plants growing under bright lights. Elsewhere in the house, police found equipment to cut and package the plants. That type of operation can yield big profits to the grower. Each plant is capable of yielding four thousand dollars' worth of marijuana, meaning that the 680 plants found in the Coldwater Creek basement were worth nearly $3 million. "[Marijuana growers] can go in and basically fly under the radar," says DEA agent Ruth Porte-Whipple. "These aren't neighborhoods where they would stand out."[50]

Moving marijuana crops indoors has become a major trend in the pot business. In 2006 the DEA seized more than 400,000 marijuana plants from indoor growing operations—an increase of 130,000 plants over the year before. Despite the increase, the DEA reports that most pot is still grown outdoors; the agency estimates that marijuana grown indoors accounts for just 10 percent of the pot produced in the United States.

Plan Mexico

Congress has responded to these trends by making drug enforcement a national priority. In 2008 Congress appropriated more than $2 billion just for the budget of the DEA. In addition, state and local governments also spend hundreds of millions of dollars on drug enforcement activities. The money helps outfit local police with electronic surveillance equipment, provides overtime pay to police officers for manning stakeouts and to undercover officers working on round-the-clock cases, pays street money to informants, and provides cash for numerous other details involved in putting together drug cases.

A HAMMER

"We don't appeal to their sense of civility and morality. We get a hammer over their heads. They realize that cooperating is the only way they can get out from under these hefty federal sentences."

U.S. attorney Rod Rosenstein, on how he coaxes testimony out of reluctant witnesses in drug cases. Quoted in Jeremy Kahn, "The Story of a Snitch," *Atlantic*, April 2007, p. 80.

Indeed, Congress and the state legislatures are continually looking for ways to strengthen the laws against drug dealing. For example, in 1986, prompted by the death of Len Bias, Congress passed the Anti-Drug Abuse Act, setting mandatory-minimum sentences for people convicted of dealing drugs. In passing the law, Congress also appropriated huge sums of money for additional antidrug law enforcement measures, including $97 million to build new prisons. Other measures adopted by the federal government include the 1998 Brownsville Agreement, in which American and Mexican authorities agreed to share in-

In 2007, George W. Bush proposed an antidrug program called Plan Mexico to Mexican president Felipe Calderon. The two leaders hoped to curb the drug trade from Mexico into the United States.

telligence about drug activities on both sides of the border, and the 2000 Plan Colombia program. In 2007 President George W. Bush proposed a new antidrug program aimed at helping Mexico root out traffickers. Dubbed "Plan Mexico," the program would provide Mexican authorities with hundreds of millions of dollars to aid police. The United States has also offered military equipment, including helicopters, to assist in the program.

At the time Bush proposed Plan Mexico, that country was in the midst of a long-running turf war among traffickers that had cost the lives of some three thousand people, most of them low-level criminals. Henry Cuellar, a congressman from Texas, said he would support the initial investment of hundreds of millions of dollars into Plan Mexico, with the understanding that the program's budget could eventually grow into the billions—as it has for Plan Colombia. According to Cuellar, "If we're going to be successful in cutting out this cancer over there, we're going to have to invest a large amount."[51]

Opposing the Drug War

While law enforcement authorities concentrate their efforts on stemming the flow of drugs over the Mexican border, traffickers have found ways to bring their drugs across the Canadian border. As police start using helicopters to find marijuana fields, growers move their operations indoors. It seems that whenever authorities conceive of a way to stifle the drug trade, the traffickers come up with new ways to thwart the police. Many critics look at the resilience of drug traffickers to deliver their product as well as the billions spent on enforcement, and wonder whether it is worth it.

Critics of the drug war suggest that the money the government pours into Plan Colombia and similar international efforts can be better spent in America on intervention programs to convince young people to stay off drugs as well as rehabilitation programs to help former users stay clean. According to the *Rolling Stone* analysis, 63 percent of all the money spent on the drug war by the United States, some $8.4 billion a year, is spent on law enforcement either in America or in other countries. The rest of the money, about $4.8 billion, is spent on treatment programs for drug abusers as well as drug prevention programs. One believer in shifting focus from law enforcement to prevention and rehabilitation is Lee Brown, the former head of the White House Office of National Drug Control Policy. Brown says, "I saw how little we were doing to help addicts, and I thought, 'This is crazy. This is how we should be breaking the cycle of addiction and crime, and we're just doing nothing.'"[52]

Moreover, opponents of the drug war believe that most people arrested in the United States are not major traffickers but rather small-time dealers or individual users. "Taxpayers spend between $7.5 and $10 billion annually arresting and prosecuting individuals for marijuana violations," says Allen St. Pierre, executive director of the National Organization for the Reform of Marijuana Laws (NORML). "Almost 90 percent of these arrests are for marijuana possession only. This is a clear misapplication of the criminal sanction and a tremendous waste of fiscal resources."[53]

Opponents of the drug war have been able to convince few political leaders of the notion that it is foolish to continue spending billions of dollars each year on rounding up drug traffickers, prosecuting them, and throwing them in jail. In America, no politician wants to be accused of being soft on crime.

SHOULD DRUGS BE LEGALIZED?

Given the overwhelming cost of the drug war as well as the limited results that have been produced over the years, some people argue that drugs should be legalized. Legalization would allow the government to control distribution, ensure the safety and purity of the substances, and even generate tax revenue from their use. Others oppose outright legalization but suggest that criminal laws are too harsh on individual users and that some forms of drug use should be decriminalized, meaning that penalties would be reduced or virtually eliminated.

A poll commissioned in 2002 by the National Organization for the Reform of Marijuana Laws found that 61 percent of Americans oppose arresting and jailing marijuana smokers. Indeed, many people equate the laws against drugs with the Eighteenth Amendment to the U.S. Constitution, the largely unsuccessful law that prohibited the manufacture and sale of alcohol. Among the ranks of those supporting decriminalization are Norm Stamper, the former police chief of Seattle, Washington. Stamper contends, "Prohibition doesn't work."[54]

NOT HARMING OTHERS

"I shouldn't be considered a criminal to have my choice. As long as I'm not harming others, I should be able to do it."

Bill Bohns, a cancer patient from Salem, Massachusetts, who supports the use of medicinal marijuana. Quoted in Taryn Plumb, "Changes Sought in Marijuana Laws, but Police Warn That Marijuana Use Isn't Harmless," *Boston Globe*, February 10, 2008. www.boston.com/news/local/articles/2008/02/10/changes_sought_in_marijuana_laws.

Meanwhile, many people also favor the legalization of marijuana for medicinal purposes. Although it has been proven that marijuana use can cause adverse effects on people's lungs as well as their long-term memories, there is no arguing with the drug's powers as an analgesic. Many people who suffer from cancer, AIDS, and other painful diseases and conditions are convinced that marijuana is an effective painkiller. Some of them have blatantly broken the law to obtain the drug.

"For me, marijuana eases the pain in my feet—on a scale of 1 to 10, it brings it from a 6 down to a 4 and keeps it there," says television talk show host Montel Williams, who suffers from multiple sclerosis, a painful nerve disease. "[Marijuana] makes it manageable so I can deal with the rest of my day. Why should it not be available?"[55]

Administrative Sanctions

Most advocates for legalizing drugs point to the success of the Netherlands (sometimes called Holland) as well as other European countries that have either legalized marijuana or have all but eliminated penalties for individuals. They insist that crime rates have dropped in those countries. In the Dutch city of Amsterdam, an adult can walk into a coffeehouse and buy a marijuana cigarette without breaking the law. It is, however, illegal to smoke pot outdoors in Amsterdam, but the city's police are known to be rather tolerant, and few people are arrested.

According to former New Mexico governor Gary Johnson, who has called for the decriminalization of drugs:

> Holland is the only country in the world that has a rational drug policy. I had always heard that Holland, where marijuana is decriminalized and controlled, had out-of-control drug abuse and crime. But when I researched it, I learned that's untrue. It's propaganda. Holland has 60 percent of the drug use—both hard drugs and marijuana—that the United States has. They have a quarter of the crime rate, a quarter of the homicide rate, a quarter the violent crime rate, and a tenth the incarceration rate.[56]

In Amsterdam, the Netherlands, people can buy marijuana legally in coffee shops like this one, which sports signs to attract English-speaking tourists.

In many foreign nations, particularly in Europe, countries have assessed the dangers of marijuana and have responded with a wide variety of laws. Indeed, what is legal in one country may be illegal in another. In Belgium, for example, marijuana use is illegal, but police have been instructed not to arrest a user unless he or she is causing a public disturbance. In the Czech Republic, it is permissible to possess a small amount of marijuana for personal use, but dealers are prosecuted. In Germany, a conviction for possession of marijuana can carry a prison sentence of five years. In Greece, the penalty is one year in jail. In Norway and Luxembourg, possession of a small amount of marijuana is punishable by fines only.

Some countries do not regard possession of a small amount of marijuana as a crime, but they still desire to levy punishments on users. Therefore, they have enacted "administrative sanctions" on people caught in possession of pot. Administrative sanctions may include suspension of a driver's license or the requirement for the user to report to police headquarters every day. Among the European nations that levy administrative sanctions are Italy, Portugal, and Spain. Author Brian Preston, whose book *Pot Planet* examines international drug laws, explains that "Spanish legal tradition is non-intrusive. It gives great respect to an individual's right to privacy, which makes the state reluctant to prosecute people who are growing a few plants for personal consumption."[57]

Marijuana in Jamaica

For decades, marijuana has been a widely used drug in Jamaica. The drug, which is known as *ganja* on the island, holds religious significance for the island's large population of Rastafarians, who believe marijuana opens their minds and helps them worship their god, Jah Rastafari. Despite the drug's overt use by as much as 40 percent of the island's 2.6 million people, marijuana use on the island is illegal.

In 2001 Jamaica's National Commission for Ganja recommended that the government legalize private use and possession of small quantities of the drug. The Jamaican parliament held hearings on the issue but ultimately decided not to legalize marijuana. Jamaican political leaders were pressured to keep the island's drug laws intact by American diplomats, who feared that legalizing the drug would encourage more exports of Jamaican marijuana to the United States.

Proponents of legalization argue, though, that Jamaican courts are clogged with marijuana cases and that the country faces much more pressing dangers from other drugs. "*Ganja* offenses have clogged up the court system for years, and diverted the police from the real problems, which are crack and cocaine," says Paul Burke, a leader of Jamaica's People's National Party and a proponent of legalizing marijuana on the island.

Quoted in Yves Colon, "Sentiment Growing Throughout Hemisphere to Legalize Marijuana," *Miami Herald*, August 18, 2001.

In most European countries, the lenient laws apply only to marijuana use. Abusers of harder drugs such as cocaine, heroin, and ecstasy typically face criminal prosecution and stiff penalties.

State Laws Vary

In America, federal laws prohibit illicit drug use, but they are largely aimed at big-time traffickers. Typically, the DEA does not concern itself with arresting people for possession of small quantities. However, all state governments have enacted laws regarding the possession, manufacture, and sale of illicit drugs. Some are quite strict, but others are very lenient—at least when they apply to possession. For example, in Kentucky, Maryland, and Arkansas, a first-time offense for possessing a small amount of marijuana could carry a year in prison. (Those laws do not necessarily mean a judge will send a first-time offender to prison for a year; most judges are lenient and likely to sentence first-time offenders to probation.) On the other hand, states such as California, Minnesota, Oregon, and Nevada have decreed no possibility of jail time for first-time offenders and require only fines to be paid if the defendants are convicted. With harder drugs, though, penalties are typically stiffer and judges less lenient, particularly for people caught selling drugs. In California, for example, somebody who sells marijuana could face up to four years in prison. In Maryland, the penalty for selling drugs is five years in prison; if police apprehend the dealer selling drugs within 1,000 feet (304m) of a school, the penalty could be as much as twenty years in prison.

Many state legislatures continually study their drug laws and question whether they are appropriate. Some states have decriminalized drugs, making possession of a small amount of marijuana a civil offense, meaning that defendants are not prosecuted in criminal court, although they may have to pay small fines if found in violation of the state's narcotics statutes. The states that have made marijuana possession a civil offense are Maine, New York, Ohio, North Carolina, Mississippi, Nebraska, and Alaska. Three other states, including New Hampshire, Vermont, and Massachusetts, are also considering statutes declaring possession of a small amount of marijuana a civil offense.

An activist demonstrates against the high numbers of nonviolent citizens in jail for drug use.

In Massachusetts, the penalty for a first-time offender caught in possession of a small amount of marijuana could be as much as six months in prison and a five-hundred-dollar fine. The proposal under consideration in Massachusetts would simply penalize marijuana users by making them pay small fines. Says Massachusetts decriminalization advocate Whitney Taylor, "Creating a civil penalty system instead of a criminal one would save Massachusetts millions of dollars in law enforcement resources, and it's been proven that decriminalization does not increase marijuana use."[58]

Meanwhile, efforts continue in other states. In Texas, where a first-time offender could face up to six months in jail for possessing a small amount of pot, the campaign to change the state's marijuana laws is led by Mark Stepnowski, a former lineman for the Dallas Cowboys. Stepnowski has admitted to regular use of marijuana since the age of fourteen. "We're trying to get marijuana reclassified so people can pay a ticket instead of going to jail," says Stepnowski, president of the Texas chapter of NORML. "The punishment does not fit the crime."[59]

Common in Society

The movement to decriminalize marijuana may be gaining traction largely because pot has become so common in American society. According to NORML, some 94 million Americans, or about 40 percent of the population of the United States, have tried marijuana at least once. In many places, people have become much more open about using the drug. Betsy Wise, a freelance advertising writer, says that when she visited a New York advertising agency on an assignment, she discovered that one of the employees brought in pot-laced brownies. "When I got to the agency, all but a few of the brownies were gone," she says. "Pretty much everyone partook, right in the office. They all greeted me with smiles. I thought that was remarkable."[60]

Certainly, most businesses do not condone the use of marijuana on the job, just as they would not condone using alcohol at work. Still, the open use of the drug in the advertising agency's office shows that attitudes about marijuana use are often relaxed. According to Jenji Kohan, the creator of the television comedy series *Weeds*—which tells the story of a middle-class mother who sells pot to make ends meet—"I think there is more of a laissez-faire attitude these days about smoking pot."[61]

Howard Finkelstein, a lawyer from Broward County, Florida, says that people who obtain marijuana for their personal use are not criminals—they are simply people who want to enjoy a drug that affects no one but themselves. "We're making war on our own people," Finkelstein insists. "We take good fathers and lawyers and doctors and wives and make them outlaws."[62]

Marijuana Vending Machines

In California about two hundred stores and similar dispensaries have been licensed by the state to sell marijuana to patients who have prescriptions from their doctors to use the drug for medicinal purposes. To make it easier for his customers to obtain their pot, Vincent

This vending machine in Los Angeles dispenses marijuana for medical use. Those who qualify for legal medical marijuana must use an ID card and fingerprint.

Mehdizadeh has installed marijuana-dispensing vending machines in the two Los Angeles stores he owns.

To use the machines, customers must have store-issued identity cards. The machines also require fingerprint verification to dispense the drug. The machines are equipped with cameras, which photograph each buyer at the time of purchase.

According to Mehdizadeh, the machines offer convenience, privacy, and speed to patients who prefer to buy their marijuana anonymously rather than deal with a store clerk. Another retailer that employs a vending machine is the Timothy Leary Medical Dispensary in Los Angeles. Store employee Robert Schwartz says, "It helps a lot of patients who are in a lot of pain and don't want to wait around to get help. It's been working great."

Quoted in Daisy Nguyen, "Pot Vending Machines in L.A.," Associated Press, January 30, 2008. http:// ap.google.com/article/ALeqM5hiL8dtDwoW4iYiA0h PDjgTkkP3wD8UG58V00.

Allen St. Pierre, the national director of NORML, has called for Congress and the state legislatures to take a much different approach to marijuana. Instead of regarding pot as an illegal drug, or even decriminalizing the use of marijuana, St. Pierre believes the government should legalize the drug and enact standards that would regulate its growth and distribution. St. Pierre also suggests that the government could levy heavy taxes on its use, much the way the federal and state governments tax the sale of alcohol and tobacco products. According to St. Pierre:

> Some 94 million Americans acknowledge having used marijuana during their lives. It makes no sense to continue to treat nearly half of all Americans as criminals for their use of a substance that poses no greater—and arguably far fewer—health risks than alcohol or tobacco. A better and more sensible solution would be to tax and regulate cannabis in a manner similar to alcohol and tobacco.[63]

THE WAR ON CITIZENS

"In declaring war on drugs, we've declared war on our fellow citizens. War requires 'hostiles'—enemies we can demonize, fear and loathe. This unfortunate categorization of millions of our citizens justifies treating them as dope fiends, less than human."

Norm Stamper, the former police chief of Seattle, Washington. Norm Stamper, "Legalize Drugs—All of Them," *Seattle Times*, December 4, 2005. http://seattletimes.nwsource.com/html/opinion/2002661006_sunstamper04.html.

Medicinal Marijuana Debate

While the debate continues over decriminalization of marijuana for recreational use, there is a solid bloc of support for legalizing marijuana for medicinal use. For years people who suffer from cancer and other painful diseases have called on the states as well as the federal government to permit them to use marijuana to ease their symptoms. In addition to providing pain relief, proponents of medicinal marijuana also insist that the drug makes them feel better about themselves and helps relieve depression over their physical ailments. Also, proponents suggest, marijuana's propensity for making users hungry can help restore strength in people whose illnesses rob them of their appetites. They suggest that AIDS patients could greatly benefit from marijuana use since AIDS often saps patients of their strength. By eating better and maintaining their strength, they argue, AIDS patients can better fight the disease.

The use of marijuana for medicinal purposes actually has a very long history. In 1937, when Congress passed the Marijuana Tax Act, pharmaceutical companies won an exemption permitting them to continue to use extract of cannabis in painkillers. At the time, some thirty medications containing marijuana extract were on the market. (Eventually, those medications were phased out and were finally banned in 1970 with the adoption of the Controlled Substances Act.)

But even after those drugs dropped out of the marketplace, people in pain have continued to find relief in pot. As Jack Branson, a Denver, Colorado, man who has suffered from AIDS for more than twenty years, explains, "Physically, it helps with the

An employee of a medicinal cannabis shop prepares joints for sale. The state of California allows the use of medical marijuana with a prescription.

nausea and my appetite. It's the only way I can keep food down and my medications. Plus, I'm able to focus a little better. Rather than being so anxious and depressed about my prognosis, I think about what I need to do to try and survive rather than always feel the anxiety of dying."[64]

Sympathy for Their Plight

Activists like Branson have found a degree of sympathy for their plight among state legislators. Over the years, twelve states have passed laws giving permission to doctors to write prescriptions for marijuana use by their patients. Typically, states that permit marijuana use for medicinal purposes issue marijuana registration cards to users, who must show their doctors' prescriptions to obtain the cards. If the user is questioned by police in a marijuana case, possession of the registration card proves that he or she has the legal right to use the drug.

States that permit medicinal marijuana use include Alaska, California, Colorado, Hawaii, Maine, Montana, Nevada, New Mexico, Oregon, Rhode Island, Vermont, and Washington. Ten more state legislatures, as well as the city council in Washington, D.C., have passed symbolic resolutions supporting the use of marijuana for medicinal purposes but have not given those measures the weight of law.

No Scientific Evidence

"To date, science and research have not determined that smoking a crude plant is safe or effective. We have a responsibility as a civilized society to ensure that the medicine Americans receive from their doctors is effective, safe and free from the pro-drug politics that are being promoted in America under the guise of medicine."

John P. Walters, director of the White House Office of National Drug Control Policy. Quoted in Linda Greenhouse, "Justices Say U.S. May Prohibit the Use of Medical Marijuana," *New York Times*, June 7, 2005, p. A-1.

Despite the support for medicinal marijuana in many state capitals, the federal government has steadfastly insisted that under the Controlled Substances Act, marijuana is a schedule I drug and, therefore, has no legitimate value. In 2002 U.S. attorney general John Ashcroft initiated a crackdown on medicinal marijuana, dispatching DEA agents to arrest growers. That year, the DEA arrested Diane Monson in Oroville, California, who had been growing pot in her backyard to relieve her chronic back pain. Monson fought back, filing a lawsuit against the Justice Department, claiming that the federal government could not enforce the Controlled Substances Act in states that had adopted laws permitting the use of medicinal marijuana. Monson was joined in the lawsuit by Angel Raich of Oakland, California, who used medicinal marijuana to alleviate her suffering from a brain tumor and a condition known as wasting syndrome, which requires her to consume food every two hours. "I don't know how to explain it," Raich says. "I just can't swallow without cannabis."[65]

In 2005 the case filed by Monson and Raich found its way to the U.S. Supreme Court, whose members expressed sympathy for people who live with pain but, in a six-to-three decision, ruled that legalizing marijuana for medicinal use would pave the way for a sweeping legalization of the drug for recreational use. The Court also found that numerous legal painkillers are available to consumers. In fact, one prescription painkiller, Marinol, is composed of a synthetic form of THC—the ingredient of pot that gives the drug its narcotic effect. Still, the Court did not throw out the state laws permitting legalization of medicinal marijuana. It simply said that federal agents could pursue prosecutions against users and growers. In those states that have legalized the medical use of the drug, the Court ruled, the local and state police could not prosecute people with a doctor's permission to use the drug. Since it is the local and state police who typically arrest individual users—and not the DEA—the Court's ruling essentially cleared the way for patients in medical marijuana states to continue using the drug.

The Court also ruled that Congress could change the law legalizing marijuana use for medical purposes on a national scale, and it suggested that advocates take their pleas to Capitol Hill. Not all justices agreed with the decision. In her opinion supporting a blanket legalization of medicinal marijuana, former Supreme Court justice Sandra Day O'Connor said the states should

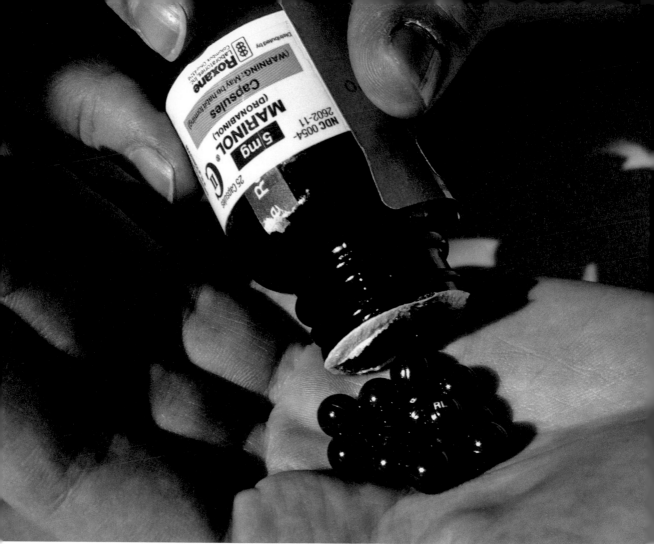

The prescription painkiller Marinol is made of a synthetic form of THC, the ingredient in marijuana that causes its narcotic effect.

have the right to decide what is best for their citizens. According to O'Connor, "[There is] an express choice by some states, concerned for the lives and liberties of their people, to regulate medical marijuana differently."[66]

Studying and Evolving

Under the ruling, the federal government was given permission to continue pursuing sellers and users of medicinal marijuana in all the states, including those that have legalized the drug for medical use. Since the ruling, however, federal agents have prosecuted few medicinal marijuana cases, prompting advocates to continue their push for laws supporting medical use of the drug.

As Bruce Merkin, the communications director for the Marijuana Policy Project in Washington, D.C., explains:

> What this ruling does is maintain the status quo. The Supreme Court has simply said that people protected under state laws can be prosecuted by federal authorities, but the state and local protections remain intact. Nothing really changes except that medical marijuana users now face the remote chance that federal agents and prosecutors will have time to prosecute a relative handful of legitimate users.[67]

Indeed, since the 2005 Supreme Court ruling, the states that legalized medicinal marijuana have kept their laws intact and other states have considered joining their ranks. In fact, New Mexico adopted its law permitting the use of medicinal marijuana after the Supreme Court ruling. Other states have also indicated a willingness to legalize pot for medical purposes. In 2007, then–New York governor Eliot Spitzer said he would support legislation legalizing marijuana for medicinal use. Spitzer, a former state attorney general, said that at first he opposed legalizing the drug but a number of very ill people convinced him to rethink his position. "You learn, you study, you evolve," said the former governor. "I met with a fair number of people and there were people whose judgment I respect."[68]

In addition, more and more physicians are starting to change their thinking about medicinal marijuana. In 2008 the American College of Physicians (ACP)—an advocacy group representing some 124,000 American doctors—called on the federal government to cease prosecuting doctors who prescribe marijuana to their patients. The organization also called on the federal government to encourage more studies of medicinal marijuana. David C. Dale, the president of the ACP, states that "in terms of advocating for the public good and the good of medicine, this was the right thing to do. We recognize that this is a drug that may be able to help and harm, but the prejudices of the past shouldn't limit research into the good it can do."[69]

There is no question that public opinion supports legalization of marijuana for medical purposes. In 2004 a poll commissioned by the American Association of Retired Persons (AARP) found that 72 percent of people over the age of forty-five believed that medicinal marijuana should be made legal.

Many Challenges Ahead

On the national level, though, political leaders are hesitant to back legalization of drugs for any purpose, including medicinal. The proposal has never enjoyed more than just lukewarm support in Congress. Many political leaders continue to believe that legalizing or decriminalizing illicit drugs is bad policy, and that drugs lead only to the ruin of people's lives. According to DEA administrator Karen Tandy:

> Drug abuse remains a very serious problem facing our country. The most recent data available from the federal Centers for Disease Control and Prevention sadly reveals that in 2004, 30,711 Americans died from drug abuse. This is almost 2,000 more deaths than occurred in 2003. Compounding the loss of lives is the damage from increased crime and violence, the powerful grip of addiction, lower productivity in the workforce, child abuse and neglect, environmental danger, and the grief of lost promise. Taken together, the effect of these human tragedies eclipses even the very tragic impact of terrorism.[70]

MARIJUANA IS ADDICTIVE

"Science has shown that marijuana can produce adverse physical, mental, emotional and behavioral changes and—contrary to popular belief—it can be addictive."

Nora Volkow, director of the National Institute on Drug Abuse. Quoted in Lydia Martin and Fred Tasker, "Marijuana's Double Standard Persists," *Miami Herald*, June 4, 2007.

The comments made by Tandy as well as by marijuana proponents like Mark Stepnowski, Angel Raich, and Allen St. Pierre illustrate that when it comes to drug abuse, Americans will never be in agreement. After decades of dealing with addiction, fighting the drug war, and trying to convince young people to stay away from narcotics, drug abuse remains a major issue in the lives of many Americans—with many calling for the legalization of marijuana while others oppose legalization under any circumstances.

After all this time, it does not seem as though there has ever been an effective strategy for keeping drugs out of the country, weaning abusers off their addictions, or even convincing many people that drugs are bad for them. Certainly, as the debate over legalization of marijuana continues, and as new drugs find their way into the homes of Americans, there will be many new challenges for drug enforcement officers and, as history has often proven, many failures as well.

Introduction: The National Tragedy of Drug Abuse

1. Quoted in U.S. Substance Abuse and Mental Health Services Administration, "New National Survey Reveals Drug Use Down Among Adolescents in U.S.—Successes in Substance Abuse Recovery Highlighted," September 6, 2007. www.samhsa.gov/newsroom/advisories/070943102.aspx.

2. Quoted in Michael D. Lemonick and Alice Park, "The Science of Addiction," *Time*, July 16, 2007, p. 42.

3. Quoted in U.S. Substance Abuse and Mental Health Services Administration, "New National Survey Reveals Drug Use Down Among Adolescents in U.S."

4. Quoted in Ann Gerhart, "Uninhibited, Unrepentant, and Unstoppable," *Biography*, May 1997, p. 83.

Chapter One: Drug Abuse in America

5. Quoted in Larry Sloman, *Reefer Madness: A History of Marijuana*. New York: St. Martin's Griffin, 1998, p. 22.

6. Quoted in Edward M. Brecher, *Licit and Illicit Drugs: The Consumer Union Report*. New York: Consumers Union, 1972, pp. 42–43.

7. Quoted in Schaffer Library of Drug Policy, "The 1912 Hague International Opium Convention." www.druglibrary.org/schaffer/library/studies/canadasenate/vol3/chapter19_hague.htm.

8. Quoted in Sloman, *Reefer Madness*, p. 81.

9. Quoted in Yves Lavigne, *Hell's Angels*. New York: Lyle Stuart, 1993, pp. 45–46.

10. Timothy Leary, *Turn On, Tune In, Drop Out*. Berkeley, CA: Ronin, 1999, p. 5.

11. Hunter S. Thompson, *Fear and Loathing in Las Vegas*. New York: Vintage, 1989, pp. 23–24.

12. Robert Sabbag, *Snowblind: A Brief Career in the Cocaine Trade*. New York: Vintage, 1990, p. 80.

13. Quoted in Alex Tresniowski et al., "Taped in the Act," *People*, October 30, 2000, p. 151.

14. Quoted in Officer.com, "Agents Discover American-Mexico Tunnel Length of Eight Football Fields," January 27, 2006. www.officer.com/web/online/Homeland-Defense-and-Terror-News/Agents-Discover-American-Mexico-Tunnel-Length-Of-Eight-Football-Fields/8$28273.

15. Quoted in CNN, "Limbaugh Admits Addiction to Pain Medication," October 10, 2003. www.cnn.com/2003/SHOW BIZ/10/10/rush.limbaugh.

Chapter Two: How Drugs Affect the Brain, the Body, and Behavior

16. Quoted in Kathy Ehrich Dowd and Stephen M. Silverman, "Heath Ledger's Death Was Accidental Overdose," *People*, February 5, 2008. www.people.com/people/article/0,,20176284,00.html.

17. Quoted in Brecher, *Licit and Illicit Drugs*, p. 274.

18. Olivia Gordon, *The Agony of Ecstasy*. London: Continuum, 2004, p. 60.

19. National Institutes of Health, *The Science of Addiction*, April 2007, p. 18. www.nida.nih.gov/scienceofaddiction/.

20. Gordon, *The Agony of Ecstasy*, p. 68.

21. National Institutes of Health, *The Science of Addiction*, p. 19.

22. Quoted in Lemonick and Park, "The Science of Addiction," p. 42.

23. Quoted in BBC News, "Marijuana Affects Blood Vessels," February 8, 2005. http://news.bbc.co.uk/1/hi/health/4244489.stm.

24. Quoted in David J. Jefferson, "America's Most Dangerous Drug," *Newsweek*, August 8, 2005, p. 40.

25. Quoted in ABC News, "Cannabis Bigger Risk than Cigarettes: Study," January 29, 2008. http://abcnews.go.com/Health/CancerPreventionAndTreatment/wireStory?id=4207595.

26. Gordon, *The Agony of Ecstasy*, pp. 88–89.

27. National Institutes of Health, *The Science of Addiction*, p. 10.

Chapter Three: How Drug Abuse Affects Society

28. National Institute on Drug Abuse, "Drug Abuse and Addiction: One of America's Most Challenging Health Problems," October 25, 1999. www.nida.nih.gov/about/welcome/about drugabuse/magnitude.

29. Quoted in Jefferson, "America's Most Dangerous Drug," p. 40.

30. Quoted in Maryclaire Dale, "Judge Critical of Reids' Home," ABC News, November 2, 2007. http://abcnews.go.com/Sports/wireStory?id=3807416.

31. Quoted in Dale, "Judge Critical of Reids' Home."

32. Mark Maske, "Eagles' Struggles Produce Speculation About Reid's Coaching Future," *Washington Post*, October 4, 2007. http://blog.washingtonpost.com/nflinsider/2007/10/eagles_struggles_produce_specu.html.

33. Quoted in *Philadelphia Inquirer*, "Excerpts from *Philadelphia Magazine*," December 22, 2007. www.philly.com/philly/sports/20071222_Excerpts_from_Philadelphia_magazine.html.

34. White House Office of National Drug Control Policy, *The Economic Costs of Drug Abuse in the United States, 1992–2002*, p. vi. www.whitehousedrugpolicy.gov/publications/economic_costs/.

35. White House Office of National Drug Control Policy, *The Economic Costs of Drug Abuse in the United States, 1992–2002*, p. x.

36. Quoted in Tom Fitzgerald, "NFL Dropout Ricky Williams Chilling in Sierra," *San Francisco Chronicle*, November 21, 2004.

37. Quoted in Jim Fitzpatrick, "Marion Jones Gets 6 Months in Jail," *Time*, January 11, 2008. www.time.com/time/nation/article/0,8599,1702789,00.html.

38. Quoted in White House Office of National Drug Control Policy, "Illegal Drugs Drain $160 Billion a Year from American

Economy," January 23, 2002. www.whitehousedrugpolicy.gov/news/press02/012302.html.

39. Quoted in Vanessa Grigoriadis, "The Most Stoned Kids on the Most Stoned Day on the Most Stoned Campus on Earth," *Rolling Stone*, September 16, 2004, p. 70.

40. Quoted in Grigoriadis, "The Most Stoned Kids on the Most Stoned Day on the Most Stoned Campus on Earth," p. 70.

Chapter Four: The War on Drugs

41. Quoted in U.S. Drug Enforcement Administration, "Sandbagged! DEA Case Nets 400 Arrests, $45 Million and 18 Tons of Drugs," February 28, 2007. www.usdoj.gov/dea/pubs/states/newsrel/sd022807.html.

42. Quoted in Ben Wallace-Wells, "How America Lost the Drug War," *Rolling Stone*, December 13, 2007, p. 114.

43. Quoted in *Frontline*, "Thirty Years of America's Drug War." www.pbs.org/wgbh/pages/frontline/shows/drugs/cron.

44. Quoted in Wallace-Wells, "How America Lost the Drug War," p. 96.

45. Quoted in Laura Maggi, "Many Murders Rooted in Revenge, Drugs," *New Orleans Times-Picayune*, June 2, 2007. http://blog.nola.com/times-picayune/2007/06/many_murders_in_no_are_rooted_.html.

46. Quoted in Gwen Filosa, "Grand Jury Indictments Reinstate Charges in Two High-Profile Murder Cases," *New Orleans Times-Picayune*, August 9, 2007. http://blog.nola.com/times-picayune/2007/08/grand_jury_indictments_reinsta.html.

47. Quoted in *Burlington (VT) Free Press*, "Drug Violence Prompts Rutland Mayor to Seek Police Funding," February 6, 2008. www.burlingtonfreepress.com/apps/pbcs.dll/article?AID=/20080206/NEWS/80206018.

48. Quoted in Fox 28, "Family Finds Field of Marijuana," July 31, 2007. www.fox28.com/News/index.php?ID=22586.

49. Quoted in Joe Robinson, "Pot Growing Thrives in Parks," *Pittsburgh Post-Gazette*, August 21, 2005, p. A-12.

50. Quoted in Errin Haines, "Suburbs Becoming Hotbeds for Pot Growing; Police Find Sophisticated Setups Amid Middle-Class

Neighborhoods," *Bergen County (NJ) Record*, March 30, 2007, p. A-11.

51. Quoted in Manuel Roig-Franzia and Juan Forero, "U.S. Anti-Drug Aid Would Target Mexican Cartels," *Washington Post*, August 8, 2007, p. A-1.

52. Quoted in Wallace-Wells, "How America Lost the Drug War," p. 97.

53. Quoted in National Organization for the Reform of Marijuana Laws, "Economists Slam War on Drugs; Cost-Effectiveness of Incarceration Doubtful, National Academy of Sciences Report Says," April 12, 2001. http://norml.org/index.cfm?Group_ID=4287.

Chapter Five: Should Drugs Be Legalized?

54. Quoted in Debra J. Saunders, "Marijuana Prohibition Doesn't Work," *San Francisco Chronicle*, April 23, 2006.

55. Quoted in *USA Today*, "Montel Williams Joins Push for New Jersey Medical Marijuana Law," June 6, 2006. www.usato day.com/life/people/2006-06-06-williams-marijuana_x. htm.

56. Quoted in Brian Preston, *Pot Planet: Adventures in the Global Marijuana Culture*. New York: Grove, 2002, p. 146.

57. Preston, *Pot Planet*, p. 182.

58. Quoted in Rachel Leamon, "Marijuana Could Be Decriminalized in Massachusetts," *Boston University Daily Free Press*, January 29, 2008. http://media.www.dailyfreepress.com/media/storage/paper87/news/2008/01/29/News/Marijuana.Could.Be.Decriminalized.In.Mass-3173971.shtml.

59. Quoted in Michael O'Keeffe, "Former NFL Player Works to Change the Marijuana Laws," *New York Daily News*, May 7, 2003.

60. Quoted in Lydia Martin and Fred Tasker, "Marijuana's Double Standard Persists," *Miami Herald*, June 4, 2007.

61. Quoted in Martin and Tasker, "Marijuana's Double Standard Persists."

62. Quoted in Martin and Tasker, "Marijuana's Double Standard Persists."

63. Quoted in National Organization for the Reform of Marijuana Laws, "Marijuana Arrests for the Year 2006—829,625 —Tops Record High," September 24, 2007. http://norml. org/index.cfm?Group_ID=7370.

64. Quoted in David Harsanyi, "Medical-Marijuana User Taken on a Bad Trip by Legal System," *Denver Post*, March 29, 2007. www.denverpost.com/headlines/ci_5542663.

65. Quoted in Charles Lane, "A Defeat for Users of Medical Marijuana," *Washington Post*, June 7, 2005, p. A-1.

66. Quoted in Lane, "A Defeat for Users of Medical Marijuana," p. A-1.

67. Quoted in Rinker Buck, "Ruling Impedes Pot for the Sick; U.S. Supreme Court Delivers Setback for Medical Marijuana," *Hartford (CT) Courant*, June 7, 2005, p. A-1.

68. Quoted in James M. Odato, "Spitzer Backs Medical Marijuana: Issue Is One of Many Governor, Lawmakers Face Before Session Ends," *Albany (NY) Times Union*, June 13, 2007, p. A-3.

69. Quoted in John Sullivan, "Philadelphia Group Prescribes New Look at Pot for U.S.," *Philadelphia Inquirer*, February 16, 2008, p. A-8.

70. Karen Tandy, "Statement of Karen Tandy, Administrator of the Drug Enforcement Administration, Before the United States House of Representatives Committee on Appropriation, Subcommittee on Commerce, Justice, Science, and Related Agencies," March 22, 2007. www.usdoj.gov/dea/pubs/ cngrtest/ct032207p.html.

DISCUSSION QUESTIONS

Chapter One: Drug Abuse in America

1. What were some of the factors that prompted Congress to adopt the U.S. Pure Food and Drug Act in 1906?

2. What were some of the social changes that occurred during the 1960s that prompted many young people to experiment with drugs?

3. According to the author, how have OxyContin and similar prescription painkillers been formulated that make them prime targets for drug abusers?

Chapter Two: How Drugs Affect the Brain, the Body, and Behavior

1. What are some of the ways that drugs affect neurotransmitters and receptors?

2. How does the brain react to pleasurable experiences?

3. What are some of the ways in which marijuana use has been compared to cigarette smoking?

Chapter Three: How Drug Abuse Affects Society

1. What are some of the ways in which drug abuse has had an economic impact on American society?

2. According to the author, what is the main question asked by fans when they learn that some of the biggest stars in sports use performance-enhancing drugs?

3. Why is the date April 20 significant in the drug culture?

Chapter Four: The War on Drugs

1. In 1973 the new U.S. Drug Enforcement Administration drew agents from the U.S. Customs Service and the Central

Intelligence Agency. How did these agents and the new organization change the scope of the drug war?

2. Why is it so difficult to convince witnesses to testify in drug cases?

3. Each year more than $8 billion is spent to investigate and prosecute drug cases. How do opponents of the drug war believe this money could be better spent?

Chapter Five: Should Drugs Be Legalized?

1. What are some of the rationales offered by advocates who propose the decriminalization of marijuana?

2. What are some of the lesser penalties faced by marijuana users in states as well as foreign countries that have decriminalized pot?

3. What qualities of marijuana have prompted people with cancer and other painful diseases to use the drug for medicinal purposes?

ORGANIZATIONS TO CONTACT

Crystal Meth Anonymous
8205 Santa Monica Blvd.
West Hollywood, CA 90046-5977
phone: (213) 488-4455
Web site: www.crystalmeth.org

This national organization coordinates chapters in more than fifty cities in the United States and Canada, where former meth users meet regularly to help one another stay clean. A national convention is held annually in Los Angeles. Its Web site provides links to the local chapters.

Drug Enforcement Administration (DEA)
2401 Jefferson Davis Hwy.
Alexandria, VA 22301
phone: (202) 307-1000
Web site: www.usdoj.gov/dea

The U.S. Justice Department's chief antidrug law enforcement agency is charged with investigating the illegal narcotics trade in the United States and helping local police agencies with their antidrug efforts. The DEA's Web site includes many reports on efforts by the agency to break up drug rings.

European Monitoring Centre for Drugs and Drug Addiction
Rua da Cruz de Santa Apolónia 23–25
PT-1149-045 Lisbon, Portugal
phone: (+351) 21 811 3000
fax: (+351) 21 813 1711
e-mail: info@emcdda.europa.eu
Web site: http://eldd.emcdda.eu.int

Based in Portugal, the organization monitors narcotics use in Europe Visitors to the Web site can download the report "Decriminalization in Europe? Recent Developments in Legal Approaches to Drug Use," which provides a breakdown of how each country in Europe tolerates marijuana use.

Narcotics Anonymous
PO Box 9999
Van Nuys, CA 91409
phone: (818) 773-9999
fax: (818) 700-0700
e-mail: fsmail@na.org
Website: www.na.org

Established in the 1950s, Narcotics Anonymous supports more than twenty thousand groups in America and some one hundred foreign countries, which hold more than thirty thousand weekly meetings a year. The meetings serve as forums for members to help one another emerge from their addictions.

National Drug Intelligence Center (NDIC)
319 Washington St., 5th Fl.
Johnstown, PA 15901-1622
phone: (814) 532-4601
fax: (814) 532-4690
e-mail: ndic.contacts@usdoj.gov
Web site: www.usdoj.gov/ndic

Part of the Justice Department, the agency provides intelligence on drug trends to government leaders and law enforcement agencies. Each year the NDIC produces the *National Drug Threat Assessment*, which includes information on illicit drug use in America.

National Institute on Drug Abuse (NIDA)
6001 Executive Blvd., Rm. 5213
Bethesda, MD 20892-9561
phone: (301) 443-1124
e-mail: information@nida.nih.gov
Web site: www.nida.nih.gov

Part of the National Institutes of Health, NIDA's mission is to help finance scientific research projects that study addiction trends and treatment of chronic drug users.

National Organization for the Reform of Marijuana Laws (NORML)

1600 K St. NW, Ste. 501
Washington, DC 20006-2832
phone: (202) 483-5500
fax: (202) 483-0057
e-mail: norml@norml.org
Web site: www.norml.org

NORML's Web site contains news, position papers, statistics, and reports on marijuana use in America. Students can find a state-by-state breakdown of marijuana laws and the legal penalties faced by offenders.

Partnership for a Drug-Free America

405 Lexington Ave., Ste. 1601
New York, NY 10174
phone: (212) 922-1560
fax: (212) 922-1570
Web site: www.drugfreeamerica.org

Funded by American corporations and media organizations that provide free advertising space, the partnership helps convince young people to stay away from drugs.

Substance Abuse and Mental Health Services Administration

1 Choke Cherry Rd., Rm. 8-1054
Rockville, MD 20857
phone: (240) 276-2000
fax: (240) 276-2135
Web site: www.samhsa.gov

An agency of the U.S. Department of Health and Human Services, the Substance Abuse and Mental Health Services Administration helps develop programs for people who are at risk to become drug abusers and assesses the spread of drug use in American society.

White House Office of National Drug Control Policy

Drug Policy Information Clearinghouse
PO Box 6000

Rockville, MD 20849-6000
phone: (800) 666-3332
fax: (301) 519–5212
Web site: www.whitehousedrugpolicy.gov

The White House Office of National Drug Control Policy was established to develop a national strategy to combat illegal drug use. The office serves as a liaison among the different federal drug investigation and research agencies and helps provide information to state and local agencies that fight drug abuse.

Books

Olivia Gordon, *The Agony of Ecstasy*. London: Continuum, 2004. The teenager relates how she became addicted to ecstasy and what she had to do to break away from the club-drug party scene.

Timothy Leary, *Turn On, Tune In, Drop Out*. Berkeley, CA: Ronin, 1999. The LSD guru from the 1960s uses a generous dose of humor to argue that psychedelic drugs can expand the mind.

Robin Moore, *The French Connection: A True Account of Cops, Narcotics, and International Conspiracy*. Guilford, CT: Lyons, 2003. The book tells the story of how two New York City detectives smashed an international heroin smuggling ring.

Brian Preston, *Pot Planet: Adventures in the Global Marijuana Culture*. New York: Grove, 2002. The author immersed himself in the drug culture in a number of countries, including the Netherlands, Nepal, Australia, Morocco, and the United States, relating his experiences in places where drugs are tolerated by the authorities as well as places where he risked arrest and imprisonment.

Ed Rosenthal and Steve Kubby, *Why Marijuana Should Be Legal*. New York: Thunder's Mouth, 2003. The authors argue forcefully for legalization of pot, concluding that medical concerns are overstated, intervention programs are ineffective, and the war on drugs focuses too much on arresting individual users.

Robert Sabbag, *Snowblind: A Brief Career in the Cocaine Trade*. New York: Vintage, 1990. The book serves as a biography of Zachary Swan, a small-time cocaine dealer who pursues a drug deal from Colombia to the United States.

Larry Sloman, *Reefer Madness: A History of Marijuana*. New York: St. Martin's Griffin, 1998. The author traces the history of marijuana use in the United States and includes a vivid portrayal of Harry J. Anslinger's days as head of the Federal Bureau of Narcotics.

Periodicals

Vanessa Grigoriadis, "The Most Stoned Kids on the Most Stoned Day on the Most Stoned Campus on Earth," *Rolling Stone*, August 16, 2004. The author follows Moppy and Molly, two stoner students at the University of California at Santa Cruz, on the day of the April 20 "420" rally on campus.

David J. Jefferson, "America's Most Dangerous Drug," *Newsweek*, August 8, 2005. The story chronicles the rise of crystal meth in American society and relates the cases of a number of people who became addicted to the drug and how their lives were changed by their addictions.

Jeremy Kahn, "The Story of a Snitch," *Atlantic*, June 2007. The author probes the drug culture in inner-city Baltimore, Maryland, and explains the pressures on African American youths to not cooperate with police in drug investigations.

Ben Wallace-Wells, "How America Lost the Drug War," *Rolling Stone*, December 13, 2007. The article provides a chronicle of the war against drugs in America, concluding that directing billions of dollars toward stifling the cocaine trade in Colombia and Mexico has proven to be a failure.

Web Sites

Angel's Fight to Stay Alive (www.angeljustice.org). The Web site is maintained by Angel Raich, the California woman who sued the U.S. Justice Department for the right to use marijuana for medicinal purposes. Visitors to the site can read the background of the case and news about developments in cannabis as a painkiller. Also available on the site are the actual court opinions in Raich's case, which visitors can download. The list of documents includes the 2005 U.S. Supreme Court opinion rejecting Raich's arguments but upholding the rights of states to legalize medicinal marijuana.

Frontline, "Drug Wars" (www.pbs.org/wgbh/pages/frontline/ shows/drugs). This is the companion Web site to the *Frontline* documentary "Drug Wars," which chronicles the history of America's war on drugs from the 1970s to the early years of the 2000 decade. Visitors to the site can read interviews with drug agents, prosecutors, convicted drug dealers, and others who have been a part of the drug culture in America. Also available on the site are a chronology of important dates and a map of the world's major drug trafficking centers.

INDEX

White House Office of
National Drug Control
Policy, 47, 53, 54, 64
Wiley, Harvey W., 13
Williams, Montel, 74
Williams, Ricky,
50–51
Wise, Betsy, 79

Woodstock, 20

Y
Youth
percent using drugs, 7
prescription drug abuse
among, 8, 25

PICTURE CREDITS

Cover: © Comstock/Superstock

Maury Aaseng, 7

AP Images, 14, 36, 45 (insets), 55, 58, 62, 65, 68, 70, 80

© Bettmann/Corbis, 48

© Stefano Blanchetti/Corbis, 12

© Bob Daemmrich/Corbis Sygma, 78

Kevin Dietsch/UPI/Landov, 52

Stephen M. Gross/UPI/Landov, 50

© JupiterImages/ Thinkstock/Almay, 34

Caryn Levy/Allsport/Getty Images, 40

Arnaldo Magnani/Getty Images, 27

© Dion Ogust/The Image Works, 85

© Phototake Inc./Alamy, 28, 31

Bill Ray/Time & Life Pictures/Getty Images, 17

© Reuters/Corbis, 22

Santi Vasalli Inc./Hulton Archive/Getty Images, 19

Terry Schmitt/UPI/Landov, 82

Tim Shaffer/Reuters/Landov, 45 (large photo)

© Horacio Villalobos/Corbis, 75

Emile Wamsteker/Bloomberg News/Landov, 37

ABOUT THE AUTHOR

Hal Marcovitz has written more than one hundred books for young readers. A former newspaper reporter, he lives in Chalfont, Pennsylvania, with his wife, Gail, and daughters, Michelle and Ashley.